MW00322851

Tales from the

TERRIFIC REGISTER

*The Book of Pirates
and Highwaymen*

For Keziah, who wants to be a pirate when she grows up.

First published 1825
This edition first published 2010

The History Press
The Mill, Brimscombe Port
Stroud, Gloucestershire, GL5 2QG
www.thehistorypress.co.uk

© Cate Ludlow, 2010

British Library Cataloguing in Publication Data.
A catalogue record for this book is available from the British Library.

ISBN 978 0 7524 5417 7

Typesetting and origination by The History Press
Printed in India by Nutech Print Services

Tales from the

TERRIFIC REGISTER

The Book of Pirates and Highwaymen

EDITED BY
CATE LUDLOW

THE

TERRIFIC

REGISTER;

OR,

RECORD OF

Crimes, Judgments,

PROVIDENCES, AND CALAMITIES.

London:

PUBLISHED BY SHERWOOD, JONES, AND CO.
AND HUNTER, EDINBURGH.

1825.

Printed by T. Richardson, 98, High Holborn.

GOD'S REVENGE AGAINST MURDER

Editor's Note

The *Terrific Register* is part of the glorious, gruesome, sensational, shocking and downright dreadful underbelly of nineteenth-century publishing. The Victorians, who we love to picture as prudish, had an absolute mania for gore: they read papers with headlines such as 'Shocking Murder of a Wife with a Scythe!', bought hundreds of 'authentic' accounts of executions, and loved anything to do with dark deeds, adventure and the supernatural. This collection is one of the forerunners of the genre of penny bloods and dreadfuls, the epitome of this underbelly. The roots of this genre, roughly speaking, are simple: all at once printing was cheap, and everyone – including the very poorest children – could read. Children and adults, from the slums all the way upwards, wanted something exciting to thumb through. They got it in titles such as *Varney the Vampire, or, the Feast of Blood*; *History of the Pirates of All Nations*; *Sweeney Todd, The Demon Barber of Fleet Street*; *The Wild Boys of London* and so on.

All of these stories in the *Terrific Register* are (allegedly) true. Some of them are fairly surprising. None are pleasant. Whatever magazine or series of books you devoured as a child, rest assured that the child of 185 years ago felt the same about the *Terrific Register*. You won't find anything more gruesome, more hideous, more hair-raising or more downright fun to dip into.

The Book of Pirates and Highwaymen

Black-Beard, The Pirate

Thatch or Teach was the real name of this sanguinary des-
peradoe. He obtained his cognomen of Black-beard, from
that large quantity of hair, which covered his whole face.
His beard was black, which he suffered to grow to an

extravagant length; as to breadth, it came up to his eyes; he was accustomed to twist it with ribbons, in small tails, after the manner of the Ramellies wigs, and turn them about his ears: in time of action he wore a sling over his shoulders, with three brace of pistols, hanging in holsters like bandaliers; he wore a fur-cap, and stuck a lighted match on each side under it, which appearing on each side of his face, his eyes naturally looking fierce and wild, made him altogether such a figure that imagination cannot form an idea of a fury from hell to look more frightful.

If he had the look of a fury, his humours and passions were suitable to it; we shall relate two or three more of his extravagancies, by which it will appear, to what a pitch of wickedness human nature may arrive, if its passions are not checked.

In the commonwealth of pirates, he who goes the greatest length of wickedness, is looked upon with a kind of envy amongst them, as a person of extraordinary gallantry, and is thereby entitled to be distinguished by some post, and if such a one has courage, he must certainly be a great man. The hero of whom we are writing was thoroughly accomplished in this way, and some of his frolics and wickedness were so extravagant, as if he aimed at making his men believe he was a devil incarnate; for being one day at sea, and a little flushed with drink:– 'Come,' says he, 'let us make a hell of our own, and try how long we can bear it'; accordingly he, with two or three others, went down into the hold, and closing up all the hatches, filled several pots full of brimstone and other combustible matter; and set it on fire, and so continued 'till they were almost suffocated, when some of the men cried out for air; at length he opened the hatches, not a little pleased that he held out the longest.

One night, drinking in the cabin with Hands, the pilot, and another man, Black-beard without any provocation privately draws out a small pair of pistols, and cocks them under the table, which being perceived by the man, he withdrew, and went upon deck, leaving Hands, the pilot, and the captain together. When the pistols were ready, he blew out the candle, and crossing his hands, discharged them at his company: Hands, the master, was shot through the knee, and lamed for life; the other pistol did no execution.– Being asked the meaning of this, he only answered, that if he did not now and then kill one of them, they would forget who he was.

His depredations at length became so formidable, added to the terror which his known desperate character and that of his crew every where inspired, that an application was made to the lieutenant-governor of Virginia to issue a proclamation for his apprehension, and two sloops of war were fitted out under the command of Lieutenant Maynard, who was commissioned to attack him. This however could not be managed so secretly but Black-beard had intelligence of it; but either he disbelieved or despised it, for he took no care to get out of his way; but put his vessel in a posture of defence and waited the result.

The night before the engagement, he sat up and drank the whole night, with some of his own men, and the master of a merchant-man, and having had intelligence of the two sloops coming back to attack him, one of his men asked him, in case any thing should happen to him in the engagement with the sloops, whether his wife knew where he had buried his money? He answered, that nobody but himself and the devil knew where it was, and the longest liver should take all.

At length they met. Lieutenant Maynard came to an anchor, but the place being shoal, and the channel intricate, there was no getting in where Thatch lay that night: and in the morning he weighed, and sent his boat a-head of the sloops to sound, and coming within gun-shot of the pirate received his fire: whereupon Maynard hoisted the king's colours, and stood directly towards him, with the best way that his sails and oars could make. Black-beard cut his cable, and endeavoured to make a running fight, keeping a continual fire at his enemies, with his guns; Mr Maynard not having any, kept a constant fire with small arms, while some of his men laboured at the oars; Black-beard's sloop ran aground, and Mr Maynard's drawing more water that that of the pirate, he could not come near him, so he anchored with half gun-shot of the enemy; and in order to lighten his vessel, that he might run aboard, the lieutenant ordered all his ballast be thrown overboard and all the water be staved, and then weighed and stood for him; upon this, Black-beard hailed him in this rude manner: 'D——n you for villains, who are you? And from whence came you?'

The lieutenant made him answer, 'You may see by our colours that we are no pirates.' Black-beard bid him send his boat on board, that he might see who he was; but Mr Maynard replied thus; 'I cannot spare my boat, but I will come aboard of you as soon as I can, with my sloop.' Upon this, Black-beard took a glass of liquor, and drank to him in these words: 'D——n seize my soul, if I give you quarter, or take any from you.' In answer to which Mr Maynard told him, that he expected no quarter from him, nor should he give any.

By this time Black-beard's sloop fleeted, as Mr Maynard's sloops were rowing by towards him, which not being above a foot high in the waist, and consequently the men exposed, as they came near together, (there being hitherto little or no execution done on either side,) the pirate fired a broadside charged with all manner of small shot.– A fatal stroke to them! The sloop the lieutenant was in, having twenty killed or wounded, and the other sloop nine: this could not be helped, for there being no wind, they were obliged to keep to their oars, otherwise the pirate would have got away, which, it seems, the lieutenant was resolute to prevent.

After this unlucky blow, Black-beard's sloop fell broadside to the shore: Mr Maynard's other sloop, which was called the Ranger, fell a-stern, being for the present disabled, so the lieutenant finding his own sloop had way, and would soon be on board of Thatch, he ordered all his men down, for fear of another broadside, which must have been their destruction, and the loss of their expedition. Mr Maynard was the only person that kept the deck, excepting the man at the helm, whom he directed to lie down snug, and the men in the hold were ordered to get their pistols and their swords ready for close fighting, and to come up at his command; in order to which, two ladders were placed in the hatchway for the more expedition. When the lieutenant's sloop boarded the other, captain Thatch's men threw in several new-fashioned sort of grenades, viz. case-bottles filled with powder, and small shot, slugs, and pieces of lead or iron, with a small quick match in the mouth of it, which being lighted outside, presently runs into the bottle to the powder, and as it is instantly thrown on board, generally does great execution, beside putting all the crew into a confusion; but by good Providence they had not that effect here; the men being in the hold, and Black-beard seeing few or no hands on board, told his men, that they were all knocked on the head except three or four, and therefore, says he, 'let's jump on board and cut them to pieces.'

Whereupon, under the smoke of one of the bottles just mentioned, Black-beard enters with fourteen men over the bows of Maynard's sloop, and were not seen by him 'till the air cleared; however, he just then gave a signal to his men, who all rose in an instant, and attacked the pirates with as much bravery as ever was done upon such an occasion: Black-beard and the lieutenant fired the first pistols at each other, by which the pirate received a wound; and then engaged with swords, 'till the lieutenant's unluckily broke, and stepping back to cock a pistol, Black-beard, with his cutlass, was striking at that instant that one of Maynard's men gave him a terrible wound in the neck and throat, by which the lieutenant came off with a small cut over the fingers.

They were now closely and warmly engaged, the lieutenant and twelve men against Black-beard and fourteen, 'till blood ran out of the scuppers in streams; Black-beard received a shot in his body from the pistol that lieutenant Maynard cocked, yet still stood his ground and fought with great fury, 'till he received sixteen wounds, and five of them by shot. At length, as he was cocking another pistol, having fired several before, he fell down dead; by which time eight more out of the fourteen dropt; and all the rest, much wounded, jumped over-board, and called out for quarter; which was granted, though it was only prolonging their lives for a few days. The sloop Ranger came up and attacked the men that remained in Black-beard's sloop with equal bravery, 'till they likewise cried for quarter.

The broadside that did so much mischief before they boarded, in all probability saved the rest from destruction; for before, Thatch had little or no hopes of escaping, and therefore had posted a resolute fellow, with a lighted match in the powder room, with commands to blow up when he should give him orders, which was as soon as the lieutenant and his men should have entered, that so he might have destroyed his conquerors: when the man found out how it went with Black-beard, he could hardly be persuaded from that rash act, by two prisoners that were taken in the hold of the sloop.

The Robber By Necessity

In the year 1662, when Paris was afflicted with a long and severe famine, Monsieur de Sallo, returning from a summer's evening walk, accompanied with only a page, was accosted by a man who presented his pistol, and in a manner far from hardened resolution, asked him for his money. M. de Sallo, observing that he came to the wrong person, and that he could obtain but little from him, added: 'I have but three pistoles, which are not worth a scuffle; so, much good may it do you with them; but, like a friend, let me tell you, you are going on in a very bad way.' The robber took them, and, without asking him for more, walked away, with an air of dejection and terror.

The fellow was no sooner gone, than M. de Sallo ordered his page to follow the robber, to observe where he went, and to bring him an account of all he should discover. The boy obeyed, pursued him through several obscure streets, and, at length, saw him change one of the pistoles and buy a large brown loaf. With this salutary purchase he went a few doors further, and, entering an alley, ascended several pairs of stairs. The boy crept up after him to the topmost story, where he saw him go into a room, which was no otherwise illuminated than by the friendly light of the moon; and peeping through a crevice, he perceived the wretched man cast the loaf upon the floor, and bursting into tears, cry out: 'There, eat your fill, this is the dearest loaf I ever bought: I have robbed a gentleman of three pistoles; let us husband them well, and let me have no more teazings; for, soon or late, these doings must bring me to ruin.' His wife having calmed the agony of his mind, took up the loaf, and cutting it, gave four pieces to four poor starving children.

The page having thus performed his commission, returned home, and gave his master an account of all he had seen and heard. Sallo, who was much moved, commanded the boy call him at five the next morning. He rose accordingly, and took the boy with him to show the way: he inquired of his neighbours the character of the man who lived in such a garret, with a wife and four children; by whom he was informed that he was a very industrious man, and tender husband, and a quiet neighbour; that his occupation was that of a shoemaker, and that he was a neat workman, but was overburdened with a family, and struggled hard to live in such dear times. Satisfied with this account, M. de Sallo ascended to the shoemaker's lodgings, and knocking at the door, it was opened by the unhappy man himself; who, knowing him at first sight to be the gentleman whom he had robbed, prostrated himself at his feet. M. de Sallo desired him to make no noise, assuring him that he had not the least intention to hurt him. 'You have a good character,' said he, 'among your neighbours: but you must expect your life will be cut short, if you are so wicked as to continue the freedoms you took with me. Hold out your hand; here are thirty pistoles to buy leather; husband it well, and set your children a laudable example. To put you out of further temptations to commit such ruinous and fatal actions, I will encourage your industry. I hear you are a neat workman; you will therefore, at this time, take measure of me and my lad for two pairs of shoes each, and he call upon you for them.'

The whole family seemed absorbed in joy: amazement and gratitude, in some measure, deprived them of speech. M. de Sallo departed, greatly moved, and with a mind replete with satisfaction at having saved a man, and perhaps a family, from the commission of guilt, from an ignominious death, and perhaps from everlasting punishment.

The Piracies And Murders Of Philip Roche

This inhuman monster had been concerned, with others, in insuring ships to a great value, and destroying them; by which means, and other rogeries he had got a little money; and being mate of a ship, was diligent enough in trading for himself between Ireland and France, so that he was in a way of getting himself a comfortable livelihood: but as he resolved to be rich, and finding fair dealings brought in wealth but slowly, he contrived to put other means in execution, and murdered several innocent persons in the prosecution of his abominable schemes.

Roche getting acquainted with one Neal, a fisherman at Cork, whom he found ready for any villaneous attempt, he imparted his design to him; who being pleased with the project, brings one Pierce Cullen and his brother into the confederacy, together with one Wise, who at first was very unwilling to come into their measures, and, indeed, had the least hand in the perpetration of what follows.

They pitched upon a vessel in the harbour, belonging to Peter Tartoue, a Frenchman, to execute their cruel intentions upon, because it was a small one, and had not a great number of hands on board, and it was easy afterwards to exchange it for one more fit for piracy; and therefore they applied themselves to the master of her, for passage to Nantz, whereto the ship was bound; and accordingly, at the beginning of November, 1721, they went aboard; and when at sea, Philip Roche, being an experienced sailor, the master of the vessel readily trusted him with the care of her, at times, while he and the mate went to rest.

The 15th of November, at night, was the time designed for the tragedy; but Francis Wise relented, and appeared desirous to divert them from their bloody purposes. Roche (sometimes called Captain) told him, that as Cullen and he had sustained great losses at sea, unless every Irishman present would assist in repairing their losses, by murdering all the French rogues, and running away with the ship, he should suffer the same fate with the Frenchman; but if all would assist, all should have a share in the booty. Upon this they all resolved alike, and Captain Roche ordered up three Frenchmen and a boy to band the top sails, the master and mate being then asleep in their cabins. The two first that came down, they beat out their brains, and threw them over-board: the other two seeing what was done, ran up to the top-mast head, but Cullen followed them, and taking the boy by the arm, tossed him into the sea; then driving down the man, those below knocked him on the head, and threw him overboard.

Those who were asleep, being awakened by the dismal shrieks and groans of dying men, ran upon deck in confusion, to enquire into the cause of such unusual noises; but the same cruelty was immediately inflicted upon them, before they could be sensible of the danger that threatened.

They were now (as Roche himself afterwards confessed) all over as wet with the blood that had now been spilt, as if they had been dipped in water, or stood in a shower of rain; nor did they regard it any more. Roche said, Captain Tartoue used many words for mercy, and asked them, if he had not used them with civility and kindness? If they were not of the same Christian religion, and owned the same blessed Jesus, and the like? But they not regarding what he said, took cords, and bound the poor master and his mate, back to back, and while that was doing, both of them begged with the utmost earnestness, and used the most solemn entreaties, that they at least allow them a few minutes to say their prayers, and beg mercy of God for the various sins and offences of their lives; but it did not move them, (although all the rest were dead, and no danger could be apprehended from those two alone) for the bound persons were hurried up and thrown into the sea.

The massacre being finished, they washed themselves a little from the blood, and searched the chests and lockers, and all places about the ship, and then sat down in the Captain's cabin, and refreshed themselves with some rum they found there, and (as Roche confessed) were never merrier in their lives. They invested Roche with the command of the ship, and calling him Captain, talked over their liquor, what rare actions they would perform about Cape Breton, Sable Isle, and the Banks of Newfoundland, whither they designed to go as soon as they had recruited their company, and got a better ship, which they proposed speedily to do.

Roche taking upon himself the command of the vessel, Andrew Cullen was to pass for a merchant, or supercargo; but then they bethought themselves, that they were in danger of being discovered by the papers in the ship, relating to the cargo, as bills of landing, &c.; therefore they erased and took out the name of the French master, and instead thereof, inserted the name of Roche, so that that it stood in the ship's papers, Peter Roche, master; that then having so few hands on board, they contrived if they met any ships, to give out, that they had lost some hands by their being washed overboard in a storm, and by that means screen themselves from being suspected of having committed some such wicked act, by reason of the small number of hands on boards; and also that they might prevail with some ship to spare them some, on consideration of their pretended disaster.

In going to Cadiz they were in distress by the weather, and being near Lisbon they made complaint to a ship, but obtained no assistance. They were then obliged to sail back for England, and put into the port of Dartmouth; but then they were in fear lest they might be discovered; therefore, to prevent that, they resolved to alter the ship, and getting workmen, they took down the mizen-mast, and built a spar deck, and made rails (on pretence that the sailors had been washed overboard) to secure the men. Then they took down the image of St Peter at the head of the ship, and put a lion in its place, and painted over the stern of the ship with red, and new named her the May Snow. The ship being so altered that they thought it could not be known they fancied themselves pretty secure; but wanting money to defray the charge of these alterations, Roche, as master of the vessel, and Andrew Cullen, as merchant, applied themselves to the officers of the customs for liberty to dispose of some of the cargo, in order to pay the workmen; which having obtained they sold fifty-eight barrels of beef, and having hired three more hands, they set sail for Ostend, and there having sold more barrels of beef, they steered their course to Rotterdam, disposed of the rest of the cargo, and took in one Mr Annesley, who freighted the ship for England; but in their passage, in a stormy night, it being very dark, they took up Mr Annesley their passenger, and threw him into the sea, who swam about the ship a long while, calling out for life, and telling them they should have all his goods, if they would receive him again into the vessel; but in vain were his cries!

After this, they were obliged to put into several ports, and hearing there was an enquiry made after the ship, Roche quitted her at Harve de Grace, and left the management to Cullen and the rest; who having shipped other men, sailed away to Scotland, and there quitted the vessel, which was afterwards seized and brought into the river Thames.

Some time after this, Philip Roche came to London, and making some claim for money he had made insurance of, in the name of John Eustace; the office was apprised of the fraud, and he was arrested and flung into the Counter from whence directing a letter to his wife, she shewed it to a friend, who discovered by it, that he was the principal villain concerned in the destruction of Peter Tartoue, and the crew. Upon this an information was given to my Lord Carteret, that the person who went by the name of John Eustace was Philip Roche, as aforesaid; and being brought down by his Lordship's warrant, he stiffly denied it for some time, notwithstanding a letter was found in his pocket, directed to him by the name of Roche; but being confronted by a Captain of a ship, who knew him well, he confessed it, but prevaricated in several particulars; whereupon he was committed to Newgate upon violent suspicion, and the next day was brought down again at his own request, confessed the whole, desired to be made an evidence, and promised to convict three men worse than himself. Two were discovered by him, who died miserably in the Marshalsea, and Roche himself was afterwards tried, (no more being taken,) found guilty of the piracy, and executed.

The Manner Of Executing
The Russian Pirates on The Volga

The Volga is, or used to be, frequently infested with pirates, who go in gangs of thirty, forty, or sometimes eighty persons; they make use of row-boats, which carry from twenty to thirty hands, and furnish themselves with fire-arms: their general practice is to board immediately; but where they apprehend a brave resistance they seldom make an attack. Hence few of the Russian merchants transport any cargo of value down the river, without a convoy. These robbers appear mostly in the spring, when the Volga being overflowed, they can the more easily escape a pursuit. The soldiers, who are occasionally sent after them, are ordered to take them alive, from the apprehension that allowing them to kill might prove fatal to

the innocent through the strong temptations to plunder with which the soldiers are actuated.

The punishment of these wretches when taken is not less dreadful than the cruelties they commit. A float is built, whereon a gallows is erected, on which is fastened a number of iron hooks, and on these they are hung alive by the ribs. The float is then launched into the stream: and the orders are given to all the towns and villages on the borders of the river, that none, upon pain of death, shall afford relief to any of the wretches: but put off the float if it runs ashore. Sometimes they are met by their partners in wickedness, who, if they have any hopes of their recovery, take them down, otherwise they put an end to their misery by shooting them; but if they are caught in these illegal acts of mercy, they are themselves hung up without the ceremony of a trial. It is said that one of these miscreants had the good fortune to disengage himself from the hook, and though naked and trembling with pain and loss of blood, he got ashore, when the first object he saw being a poor shepherd, he had the cruelty to beat out his brains with a stone, and then to take his clothes. These malefactors sometimes hang thus, three, four, and sometimes five days alive. The pain generally produces a raging fever, wherein they utter the most horrid imprecations, and implore the relief of water, or some small liquors.

Adventures of Morgan, The Prince Of Free-booters

Morgan was the son of an opulent Welch farmer; who, by the ferocity of his character, the strength of his mind, the extent and duration of his achievements, as well as by his success, has perhaps surpassed all the other freebooters.

He at first embarked as a common sailor; in which capacity he went to Jamaica, and in a short time became connected with the West Indian corsairs. By one of their commanders, an old freebooter named Mansfield (who was likewise an Englishman), he was patronised; and in a little time so distinguished himself by his brilliant actions, that Mansfield appointed him his vice-admiral, and died soon after, in 1688. This was the era of Morgan's first enterprises. None of his comrades disputed the command with him; and he shortly became possessed of the means of rendering himself, in consequence of his singular genius and intrepidity, one of the most famous chieftains of the free-booters.

After he had made some successful cruises, he persuaded his men not to squander their money foolishly, but to reserve it for great enterprises. To this suggestion many of them acceded; and, in a few months, he had a fleet of twelve sail, of various sizes, and seven hundred men; with whom he visited the southern parts of the island of Cuba, and determined to attack Puerto del Principe, which was situated in the interior of that island, at some distance from the southern coast.

It may not be irrelevant here to state a few brief notices concerning the island in question. Cuba, the largest of the Antilles, is two hundred French leagues in length, by fifty in its greatest breadth. It contains several mountains, in which are abundant mines of copper, silver, and gold. The city, which Morgan purposed to attack, was opulent, populous, and at a distance from the shore; and, till the present period, had been preserved from being plundered by the pirates.

There was on board their fleet a Spaniard, who was an expert swimmer, and who effected his escape by plunging into the sea. By this man the governor was informed of their plan. He therefore hastily took defensive measures, alarmed the inhabitants, and marched with eight hundred men to meet the free-booters. He merited a better fate. After four hours desperate fighting, his forces were completely defeated, and himself lay dead on the field of battle. The city continued to defend itself for some time; the inhabitants barricaded their homes, and fired from the windows. Their efforts were in vain. The free-booters threatened to set their city on fire, and massacre their women and children. They were constrained to surrender.

Morgan was extremely vexed to find that, during the battle, they had carried off their most valuable effects. The tortures inflicted upon them could not compel them to disclose where they had concealed them. The little that remained in the town was regularly plundered. All the Spaniards of both sexes, including even children at the breast, and also the slaves, were shut up in the church, where most of them perished with hunger. The pirates required a double ransom of them; one for their persons, if they did not wish to be transported to Jamaica; and the other for their city, if they wished to save it from total destruction. Four prisoners went into the woods, there to collect the sums exacted, either from the inhabitants or by other means. They returned soon after, with assurances that the whole should be paid; they requested only a respite of fifteen days, which Morgan granted. But on the following morning a Negro was brought to him, who was the bearer of a letter, written by the governor of Santo Yago, to some prisoners; in which he recommended them not to hurry themselves in paying the ransom, but to amuse the pirates under different pretences; and promised that he would himself shortly come in person to their assistance.

Morgan carefully concealed the contents of this letter, but announced to the prisoners that he would not wait longer than the following morning. In consequence of their representations, and under the apprehension of being continually attacked by large bodies of troops, he was content for the moment, with five hundred cattle. He took, however, six of the principal inhabitants as hostages; and the free-booters set sail.

They were extremely displeased with the inconsiderable amount of their booty, which, exclusive of some commodities, did not exceed 50,000 piasters. Disputes arose, in consequence of which a Frenchman was killed by an Englishman. The national animosities were re-excited (for the body of the free-booters consisted entirely of English and French), the two proceeded even to blows. In order to appease this tumult, Morgan ordered the murderer to be put in irons, and solemnly promised to give him up to a court of justice at Jamaica. With this act of impartial justice the French were but imperfectly satisfied. They were inconsolable for the little profit which their last expedition had produced; and they disapproved of that to which it was proposed to conduct them. Some of them wished to act themselves: they took, therefore, one of the ships on their own account, and separated with testimonies of friendship. On their departure, Morgan offered prayers for their success, and repeated his promise that the assassin should be legally punished. He kept his word; and on arrival at Jamaica, the Englishman was tried, convicted, and executed.

The divisions between the two nations continued, nevertheless, to prevail. It was difficult for men, whose language, sentiments, religion, and manners, were so widely different, long to agree: but as the English and the French were not on board the same ships, a separation became more easy. It was amicably effected. Most of the French left Morgan, chose one of their countrymen for their commander, and withdrew.

The confidence of the pirates in their chieftain was boundless: among them, the separation of the French produced but little sensation. Less mixed, they became more intimately united, and promised Morgan that they would follow him every where. They sedulously applied themselves to the procuring of new recruits at Jamaica; so that, in the course of a few weeks, they had collected nine ships of various sizes, and four hundred and sixty men, all devoted to their brave commander.

Till then, the free-booters had only landed in the Islands. Morgan conceived more extensive plans: he turned his views to the continent of America; and the great, the opulent city of Porto Bello was the place he intended to plunder.

Porto Bello, which was defended by three forts, is situated on the shore of a gulf, on the southern side of the isthmus of Panama. For the last two centuries to the present time, it has been known as the greatest mart in the world for valuable metals. At the period now referred to, it was a city of the greatest importance, and, next to Havana, the strongest place of all the Spanish possessions in America. The entrance of its port was defended by two castles, St James and St Philip, which were reputed to be impregnable, and were garrisoned by three hundred soldiers. Notwithstanding its vast circumference, the city was inhabited by only four hundred families, on account of the unwholesomeness of the climate. It contained scarcely any thing else but warehouses for articles, the proprietors of which constantly resided at Panama, which is situated at a small distance. Thence was sent to Porto Bello on mules, at certain periods of the year, the gold and silver that arrived from Peru and Mexico. The inhabitants of the first named place, though few in number, had the character of being good soldiers: and they deserved their reputation, from the valour with which they had on various occasions defended themselves.

Morgan had not communicated to any individual his design on Porto Bello, to prevent the Spaniards from obtaining any information concerning it. The pirates themselves were very far from suspecting it; and, when it was announced to them, were intimidated. The most intrepid among them shook their heads, and exclaimed against the smallness of their number, with which it was impossible to take so strong and extensive a city.

'What signifies it,' replied Morgan, 'how small our number is, if our hearts are great! The fewer we are, the more intimate will be our union and the more considerable our shares of plunder.'– This short address at once aroused their cupidity and their courage. The expedition was unanimously determined to be carried into execution.

It was accordingly executed in 1688, when the Spaniards had just concluded their treaty of peace with France, at Aix-la-Chapel. Morgan moored his ships, during the dark, at some distance from the city; a very few soldiers being left on board; the remainder went into boats and canoes, in order that they might land in silence near the port. The descent being effected, Morgan detached four men, under the command of an Englishman, who was well acquainted with the local situation, with orders to kill or bring away, without noise, the sentinel of the advanced post. Circumstances favoured the taking him prisoner. The soldier was surprised, stripped of his arms, and with his hands bound, was conducted to the commander of the Pirates; who, by means of threats, extorted from him all the information he wanted. The first of the two forts was next approached; and they reached without detection the very foot of the wall.

From thence the captive soldier was compelled, with a loud voice, to announce to his countrymen, in the name of Morgan, that if they did not instantly surrender, they should be cut to pieces. This menace produced no effect: the garrison began to fire upon them, and made a courageous resistance. The first was, notwithstanding, carried in a short time; when the free-booters, with a view to intimidate the inhabitants, thought it necessary to accomplish their threat. They therefore collected all the captive soldiers together, set fire to the powder magazine, and blew up both the fort and the garrison into the air. Without losing a moment, they marched towards the city.

Trembling with terror, the inhabitants were busily engaged in concealing a part at least of their riches, either by throwing them into the wells, or burying them in the earth. The governor, not being able to prevail upon them to defend themselves, shut himself up in the second fort, from which he commenced a terrible fire upon the pirates. These, however, attempted an assault: it lasted from day break till noon, and was frustrated.

The free-booters then tried the firing of red-hot balls against the gates of the fort. They were not more successful. These gates were almost wholly composed of iron; and, in addition to this impediment, the garrison threw down from the top of the walls so many stones, so many pots filled with powder, that the intrepid assailants could not approach without meeting with certain death. Even the headstrong

Morgan began to be doubtful of victory; when he beheld the English flag flying at a small distance from the fort he had just taken. This sight re-animated his courage, as well as that of his men. He made all the religeuse, of both sexes, quit their convents; and caused twelve ladders to be hastily made, and of sufficient width to admit twelve men abreast to mount them. The wretched religeuse were obliged to plant themselves against the walls, serving as a bulwark to the free-booters, who were marching behind them. Morgan had taken for granted that the governor would not venture to fire on his countrymen, especially on persons whom superstition must render sacred to him. These monastics also impatient of their horrible situation, amid the pangs of death, with which they were threatened, cried with all their might, and conjured the governor, in the name of all the saints, to surrender the fort, and save their lives. The pirates added yet more horror to this scene, by a menace, which in their lips was never in vain, that a general massacre should take place in the case of a longer resistance. The wall, at the foot of which the assailants presented themselves, was not lofty: the batteries of the fort were so exposed, and the free-booters were such able marksmen, that every cannon shot was followed by the death of some of the Spanish artillery men. They persisted notwithstanding in their determination of holding out against the pirates.

The governor, in particular, was alike deaf to every menace, and to the lamentations of the wretched recluses, near whom were the ladies of the city, the wives of the lower classes of people, and their children. Regardless of so many innocent victims, he ordered his artillery to fire upon this living rampart; behind which the free-booters were sheltered. To these terrible assailants his fire did but little damage; but it overthrew a vast number of monks, of female religeuse, and of women in general, before these hapless persons succeeded in applying the ladders to the walls.

The assault then became more easy to the free-booters, although they had no other arms than their pistols and sabres. In a short time they reached the summit of the wall, when they discharged a kind of earthen shot, filled with powder, upon the Spaniards, who were giving way a little, defending themselves at the same time with their pikes; but who, still persisting in their refusal to surrender, were all cut to pieces. *To be continued…*

Candid Culprit

The duke of Ossuna, Viceroy of Naples, passing through Barcelona, went on board the Cape Galley, and passing through the crew of slaves, he asked several of them what their offences were? Every one excused themselves upon various pretences; one said that he was put in out of malice, another by bribery of the judge; but all of them unjustly. The duke came at last to a sturdy little black man, whom he questioned as to what he was there for? 'My lord,' said he, 'I cannot deny but I am justly put here; for I wanted money, and so took a purse near Tarragona, to keep me from starving.' The duke, on hearing this, gave him two or three blows on the shoulder with his stick, saying, 'You rogue, what are you doing among so many honest innocent men? Get you out of their company.' The poor fellow was the set at liberty, while the rest were left to tug at the oar.

Justice Fighting Against Mercy

A young gentleman of family and fortune, but of abandoned principles, having long distinguished himself, in the reign of Charles II, by highway robberies, and other desperate acts against society, was often apprehended, and sometimes convicted; but through the interest of his friends, had always been pardoned. Many of the nobility interceded in his favour, but to no effect; the king was inexorable; he had the pen in his hand to sign the order for execution, when one of the nobility threw a copy of a pardon on the table before him. The Duchess of Portsmouth, his chief favourite, standing at his right shoulder, took his hand gently within her own, and conducting it to the paper which had the pardon written on it, led his hand while he subscribed his name, the king not making the least resistance. Shaking his head, and smiling, he threw the pardon to the nobleman who had interposed in the young man's behalf, adding, 'Take care you keep the rascal out of my reach for the future.'

When this pardon was shewn to Lord Chancellor Hyde, observing how badly the king's name were formed, he wittily remarked, 'That when his majesty signed the pardon, "Justice had been fighting with Mercy".'

Mull'd Sack

In an old work, entitled 'Portraits, &c. from the reign of Edward III. To the Revolution,' is a curious account of Mull'd Sack, alias John Cottington, so called from his drinking mull'd sack, morning, noon, and night. He was a most notorious fellow. He robbed Oliver Cromwell twice; once as he was coming out of Parliament House, and once on Hounslow Heath; and when at Cologne, he robbed King Charles II, then in his exile, of as much plate as was valued at £1,500.

Cowardice Punished By The Emperor Of Morocco

During Muley Abdullah's residence at Mequinez, a captain of a row-boat came from Salee to wait upon him. The sea-officer had returned from a cruise, in which he had taken two prizes; and was come to court to deliver to his majesty the share of the captures which is customarily rendered to government, and likewise to offer a considerable present as a token of his loyal affection.

The emperor received the present and share of the prizes with all seeming complacency and satisfaction; and the captain imagined that his services were highly approved. But the emperor had received an account, that the captain had, on his cruise, met with a French merchantman, but had declined an engagement, fearing the Christians might be too strong for him. On this information, the emperor had in his mind passed sentence on him as a coward, and only waited his arrival for execution.

The captain, highly pleased with the acceptance of his present, staid only for his formal dismissal. The emperor observing that he now expected his discharge, told him he could not dismiss him yet, as he had some business of importance to settle, which had not yet been duly adjusted. At this the captain was somewhat chagrined, and began to suspect the emperor's displeasure, but knew not what to attribute it to. The emperor, however, soon put an end to his uncertainty, by telling him, with an angry countenance, that he was determined to make him account for the loss of the French merchantman, which like a coward and a traitor, he had run away from; and that nothing but his life should answer for the fault.

During this interview, the emperor was on horseback, and the captain on foot. The emperor moved his horse about thirty paces from the victim of his resentment, and turning short around, with his lance in his hand, rode full speed towards him, and endeavoured to pierce him through the body. The captain, however, hoping to save his life, artfully evaded the thrust, and, according to the custom of the country, caught hold of the tail (which is usually a sanctuary from further punishment), imploring mercy and forgiveness in a most pathetic manner. The emperor, however, made no scruple to sacrifice the prejudice and good opinion of subjects in that point to the gratification of his revenge. Doubly exasperated by the evasion which the captain had made, he darted the lance into his body, and laid him lifeless in a minute, with no less than thirteen wounds, the least of which would have produced death.

Having thus performed the office of an executioner with his own hand, he commanded the dead body to be dragged to the market-place, and there exposed for three days, as a public monument of his vengeance on cowardice; and at the expiration of that term, to be dragged in the same infamous manner without the walls of the city, there to remain till the birds and beasts of prey or the operations of nature should have destroyed it.

The jacket of the unhappy victim was purchased by a Spanish captive, who preserved it, intending (should Providence ever grant him a release) to exhibit the thirteen holes made in it by the emperor's spear as monuments, in the face of Christendom, of Barbarian tyranny.

Adventures of Morgan, Prince of Free-booters: An Unusual Threat

Continued from page 28…
The pirates still had to carry the other fort, into which part of the garrison belonging to the first fort had retired, together with the governor. The first was of less importance than that which they had just taken, and served to defend the entrance of the harbour; but the free-booters were under the necessity of occupying it, in order that they might secure themselves free access to their ships. There was, in fact, no impediment whatever, to prevent them from plundering the city at their ease: but in order to carry off their booty, and especially to take away with safety their numerous wounded comrades, their ships were indispensably necessary.

That no time might be lost, they summoned the governor to surrender, promising him to spare all his soldiers. Cannon-shot were the answer. They had no time for consideration. This fort, like the former, was attacked sabre in hand; and its surrender was accelerated by the vanquished being compelled to direct their own cannons against its walls. The officers quitted their arms only with life. The soldiers, on the contrary, laid down theirs, and demanded quarter.

The governor, who was a Castilian, and whose name deserved to have been transmitted to posterity, continued furiously to defend himself; and, with his own hand, killed several of these robbers. His valour forced admiration: he haughtily rejected the pardon they offered him. In vain did his wife and daughter with tears conjure him to save his life.– 'I had rather,' he replied, 'die on the field of honour, than on a scaffold!' In fact, a glorious death only could terminate his valiant career. Thus Morgan found himself master of two strong castles; and this success had been obtained, without cannon, solely by four hundred men. The men and the women, as well as the wounded, were all shut up in separate enclosures.

Here the conqueror, whom it had been hitherto impossible not to admire, disappears, to give place to the ferocious man, whom we detest. Instead of causing the wounded to be dressed, he said to them with the most cruel irony,– 'your groans shall supply the place of clothing for your wounds.' His companions in arms shewed themselves worthy of him. During the following night, they amused themselves with intoxication, music, and the commission of the most horrid excesses. Those women, who opposed their brutality by the resistance of modesty, were threatened with instant death; and such as persisted fell beneath their blows, without being able to obtain the last consolations of religion, which they implored. The ensuing day was employed by the ferocious conquerors in searching after concealed treasures: great numbers of the unfortunate captives were put to the most cruel tortures, beneath which many of them expired.

While these transactions were taking place, Morgan was informed that the president of Panama, Don Juan Peres de Gusman, was collecting forces against him from every quarter. He nevertheless continued his operations with perfect security; in case of immediate danger, his retreat was rendered certain by his ships being in the vicinity. Lest, however, he should be surprised, he ordered the ruins of the two forts to be thrown up again; and placed his cannons to defend himself, in case he should be attacked: but the Spaniards left him a respite, of which he made ample use.

Thus the free-booters continued at Porto Bello without any apprehensions, for fifteen days; during which period they were actively occupied in supplying themselves with provisions, and in embarking all their booty. They might have prolonged their residence; but their insatiable gluttony had devoured so great a quantity of the necessaries of life, that they were at length compelled to support themselves almost wholly on horses' and asses' flesh. This scarcity was peculiarly fatal to the prisoners, who had no other sustenance but very small portions of that food, no bread, and some cistern water. This unwholesome and muddy fluid was, indeed, the ordinary drink of the inhabitants; but they had recourse to filtration; an expedient which was prohibited to these unfortunate persons. The robbers themselves had no other water; but this circumstance not a little contributed to hasten their departure.

But, before they quitted the place, Morgan had the audacity to send to the president of Panama two prisoners, who were ordered to demand 100,000 piasters for the ransom of Porto Bello, if he did not wish to see it reduced to ashes. The president had been able to muster only 1,500 men, which number, however, he thought sufficient to carry without delay his answer.

But these forces, though so greatly superior to those of the pirates, did not impose upon them. They marched to meet the Spaniards, occupied a defile, where they attacked them, and occasioned considerable loss among them. Gusman, who did not doubt but the reinforcements he expected would ultimately secure him the victory, was by no means discouraged at this first check; and sent to inform Morgan that nothing could save him, unless he instantly quitted Porto Bello. Morgan replied, that above all things he wished to have the ransom demanded; and that, if he did not obtain it, he certainly would embark; but that it should not be till he had burnt the city, demolished the forts, and put every prisoner to death. This terrifying answer damped the president's courage. The moment he heard of the capture of Porto Bello, he had dispatched an express to Carthagena, to press the sending of a small fleet, which was to cut off the free-booters by the sea, while he attacked them by land. But these measures, though so exceedingly urgent, were slowly carried into execution; and when the pirates were ready to set sail, no hope remained that the flotilla would arrive in time. In this situation the president left the inhabitants to save themselves, how they could. The hundred thousand piastres were speedily collected and paid.

Gusman, who had served in Flanders in the rank of general, could not but admire those free-booters, who had performed such vast exploits with so few men; and who, without undertaking a formal siege, had succeeded in taking a city defended by a wall, ramparts, and cannons. He could not conceive what arms they had made use of, in order to obtain such signal success: he therefore sent a messenger to Morgan, to carry him some refreshments; and requested him to return a specimen of his arms, as a mark of his remembrance. Morgan gave the messenger a hearty reception, and by him transmitted a pistol, together with some little balls, and thus addressed him:– 'Tell the president, if he pleases, to accept this small specimen of the arms with which I have conquered Porto Bello, and to keep it one year. At the expiration of that term, I promise to come myself to Panama, and shew him how to use it.' To his thanks, for such a promise, the president added a fine emerald set in a gold ring; but he returned his pistol and balls, with directions to inform Morgan that he did not want for arms of that sort; and advised him to spare himself the trouble of coming to Panama, as he should not there succeed so well as at Porto Bello. At the same time he could not, however, but express his regret, that such brave fellows were not in the service of some great prince, and that they could not display their singular valour in a lawful war. It may be easily conceived in what manner this frank and ingenious compliment was received by the free-booters.

At length they departed without any obstacle occurring, after they had taken away the best cannon from the forts, and had spiked the rest. They sailed first towards the island of Cuba: there they examined their plunder; which, exclusive of a great quantity of jewels and valuable articles, consisted of gold and silver, both coined and in plate, to the value of 250,000 piasters. They afterwards transported themselves, together with their treasures, to Jamaica.

These robbers were not formed for repose. In a short time they began to make preparations for a new expedition. To the veterans, who were to be engaged in it, were added a crowd of novices, more eager to participate in Morgan's plunder than in his glory. Through the protection of the governor of Jamaica, he obtained a six-and-thirty gun ship. With this reinforcement, which equally added to his military strength and importance, he departed for Hispaniola in January, 1669.

... Morgan, in the presence of all the free-booters, whose number was completed by the arrival of the other ships, disclosed his plan of sailing towards Savanna, and there to take the rich fleet which would arrive from Spain. The proposal was received with enthusiasm; cries of joy were mingled with discharges of artillery. The excesses of intoxication which covered this tumult, deprived these marauders of their reason, and lulled their vigilance to sleep.

In the midst of their drunken revels, the ship blew up into the air, and three hundred and fifty Englishmen were buried at sea. Thirty only, including Morgan, were spared, who were in a large hut, and consequently at a distance from the centre of the explosion. A few others might have saved themselves, but they were so intoxicated as to be unable to make any efforts for that purpose. By this accident three hundred and twenty pirates were lost. The survivors exerted themselves very actively in fishing them up again, – not indeed from any pious regard for the mortal remains of their comrades, but to strip them of the gold rings which these corsairs commonly wore on their fingers.

… The destruction of his principal ship was to him a very sensible loss; he had now only fifteen remaining, the largest of which carried only fourteen small cannons. He could still reckon, indeed, on board his fleet nine hundred freebooters; but he had not yet arrived at the height of his misfortunes. In one night, after various adventures, his fleet was so ill-treated by a tempest, that on the following day it was reduced to eight ships, and his little army to five hundred men. In case of a separation, it had been previously determined that they should resort to the bay of Ocos, as the point of re-union; and thither the commander-in-chief hastened, but not one of his ships appeared there.

From that time he changed his plans of operations; and by the advice of the celebrated Peter the Picard, who had been with Olonois in the expedition to Maracäibo, he determined to pay a new visit to that Spanish possession. He fortunately arrived with his men on the borders of the lake of that name, where he found that the Spaniards had recently built a fort, the artillery of which commenced and kept up a most terrible fire upon his ships. With this unexpected reception the pirates were by no means daunted; they ventured to land. Intimidated by such audacity, which recalled to the mind the first attack of the free-booters, the Spaniards rapidly evacuated the fort, and placed a lighted match near the powder magazine, in order to blow up both the fort and the pirates themselves. The plot, however, was detected by Morgan at the very moment that the explosion was about to take place. He found in the fort thirty quintals of gunpowder, several fusees and pikes, an extensive military baggage, and seventeen large cannons. A few pieces only were spiked, the remainder being carried on board the ships. The fort was demolished as far as precipitation would allow them; for it was constructed in a peculiar manner, so that it could only be ascended by an iron ladder which was drawn up as soon as the person attained the top of the wall.

But this conquest was not attended with any great utility to the free-booters. They were obliged to advance further, and they had many obstacles to surmount. The shallowness of the water compelled them to abandon their ships, and continue their navigation in canoes. But the terror with which the Spaniards were struck removed all difficulties. Their inconsiderable strength might have encouraged their enemies to make some resistance; this however was not the case. Though so valiant under other circumstances, they durst not contend with these ferocious free-booters; they abandoned not only the city of Maracäibo, but also the fort of La Barra, and betook themselves to flight. The pirates found only a few aged slaves who could not walk, and some invalids in the hospital, a very small quantity of provisions, and the houses stripped and deserted. The Spaniards had had time to secure their merchandise and moveables; they had even sent their small craft out of the port, and had conducted themselves further into the interior of the lake.

Morgan ordered the woods to be searched: in a short time there were brought in fifty mules richly laden, and thirty fugitives, men, women, and children. Conformably to the horrible custom of these robbers, they put the hapless captives to the torture, in order to extort their confessions. Their limbs were fastened to ropes, which were violently drawn in contrary directions; to their fingers were applied pieces of burning wood; their heads were tightly bound with cords, till the eyes were ready to start from their sockets. Some slaves who would not betray the place of their masters' retreat, were cut to pieces while alive. Every day were detachments sent into the woods to hunt the fugitives; and the hunters never returned without bringing in some human prey.

To be continued…

Juvenile Criminal

'Among the children,' says that active philanthropist, the Hon. Grey Bennet, in his evidence before the Police Committee, 'whom I have seen in prison, a boy of the name of Leary was the most remarkable; he was about thirteen years of age, good-looking, sharp, and intelligent, and possessing a manner which seemed to indicate a character very different from what he really possessed. When I saw him, he was under sentence of death for stealing a watch, chain, and seals, from Mr Princep's chambers in the Temple; he had been five years in the practice of delinquency, progressing from stealing an apple off a stall, to housebreaking and highway robbery.

He belonged to the Moorfields' Catholic Chapel, and there became acquainted with one Ryan in that school, by whom he was instructed in the various arts and practices of delinquency; his first attempts were at tarts, apples, &c; next at the loaves in bakers' baskets; then at parcels of halfpence on shop counters and money-tills in shops; then to breaking shop windows, and drawing out valuable articles through the aperture, picking pockets, house-breaking, &c. Leary has often gone to school the next day with several pounds in his pockets, as his share of the produce of the previous day's robberies; he soon became captain of a gang, generally since known as Leary's gang, with five boys, and sometimes more, furnished with pistols, taking a horse and cart with them; and, if they had an opportunity in their road, they cut off the trunks of gentleman's carriages, when, after opening them, and according to their contents, so they would be governed in prosecuting their further objects in that quarter; they would divide into parties of two, sometimes one, and leaving one with the horse and cart, go to the farm and other houses, stating their being on their way to see their families, and begging for some bread and water; by such tales, united with their youth, they obtained relief, and generally ended by robbing the houses and premises.

In one instance Leary was detected and taken, and committed to Maidstone gaol; but the prosecutor not appearing against him, he was discharged. In these excursions he has stayed out a week and upwards, when his share has produced him from £50 to £100. He has been concerned in various robberies in London and the vicinity, and has had property at one time amounting to £350; but when he had money, he either got robbed of it by elder thieves, who knew he had much money about him, or he lost it by gambling at flash houses, or spent it among loose characters of both sexes.

After committing innumerable depredations, he was detected at Mr Derrimore's, at Kentish Town, stealing some plate from that gentlemen's dining room; when several other similar robberies coming against him in that neighbourhood, he was, in compassion of his youth, placed in the Philanthropic Asylum; but being now charged with Mr Princept's robbery, he was taken, tried, convicted, and sentenced to death, but was afterwards respited, and returned to that Institution.

He is little, and well-looking; and has robbed to the amount of £3,000 during his five years' career. This surprising boy has since broke out and escaped the Philanthropic, went to his old practices, was again tried at the Old Bailey, and is transported for life.'

Piracy, Murder, And Rape: Part One

In the year 1735, Captain De Tracy, a Frenchman of a distinguished family, had acquired considerable wealth by his extensive plantations in the vicinity of Samana, in the island of St Domingo. He had constantly resided on one of his own estates, and had married a Creole lady of remarkable beauty and accomplishments, and was blessed by her with an early family of healthy and interesting children. De Tracy, of an open-hearted and generous disposition, uniformly conducted himself towards his slaves and dependants with kindness and affability. The family of De Tracy consisted at that time of one daughter, verging on fifteen, and a second one year older, a fine grown boy of thirteen, another of eight years old, and a smiling infant at the mother's breast. The elder daughters possessed all the personal charms, with all the gentleness of their mother; of the boys it need only be said, that they bade fair to inherit the noble-mindedness of their parents.

De Tracy, with his amiable and fair family, had resided since his marriage entirely on his principal estate in the island of St Domingo; but in the summer of the year 1735, he determined to visit the Bahama Islands, of which Madame De Tracy was a native, and where she had now become possessed of considerable property by the bequest of her father, recently deceased. A residence of some months in the Bahamas being advised to the re-establishment of Madam De Tracy's health, it was arranged that the whole family should accompany them.

In the month of January preceding, a brig, apparently designed for a vessel of war, with a mixed crew of twenty men, and commanded by a Frenchman, was driven, in a severe gale, on the coast, and, having received extensive damage, had been compelled to remain on the island for repair and refitted. Her captain described himself as a naval commander, educated in the French marine, but compelled to resort to the pursuits of commerce to repair the destruction of his early pursuits and fortune. The numbers and appearance of his crew seemed to be at variance with this account, and the vessel itself bore strong resemblance, in its sitting and general equipment, to one used for the purpose of privateering depredation, rather than the peaceful occupations of trade. The account which La Force, the commander, gave of himself, however, ran, that he was on an outward-bound voyage from Marseilles to the gulph of Florida, with a cargo of Dutch and English manufactured goods, to trade with the Spaniards; and that the unusual number of his crew arose from his having shipped, as passengers, several Spaniards, Portuguese, and Italians, who were proceeding to settle in the Spanish South-American dominions. The relation accounted tolerably well for the doubtful appearance of his men, and the presence of a number of bales and packages of every variety of sizes, marks, and denominations. The guns of his vessel, with the ammunition, and a quantity of small arms, had, in fact, been thrown overboard as a matter of necessity during the gale, as well to lighten and ease the ship, as to remove all violent cause of suspicion, from the shore on which they were inevitably driving. In few words, to relieve the suspense of the reader, the brig Julie, we are describing, was in reality a stout vessel of war, expressly fitted out by a band of adventurers who formed her desperate crew, for piracy and marauding, and previous to the storm which drove her into St Domingo, had been in a complete state of warlike readiness to grapple even with armed vessels of much superior rate; and the merchandize and valuables saved from her when stranded, were the result of many rich captures. La Force, who with courteous and specious manners glossed over the blackest heart that perhaps ever animated the human frame, was a pirate of the most determined and fearless character, and of disposition more cruel and relentless than was usual, even amongst the desperadoes of his own class.

De Tracy, in the sincerity and openness of his heart, suspected no guile in others, and in an evil hour determined to avail himself of the Julie being ready for sea, and take his projected passage to the Bahamas under the conduct of the pirate La Force and his band of miscreants. It should be told, that from the first landing of La Force from his wicked vessel, De Tracy, with his wonted kindness, had bade him a cheerful welcome to the comforts of his house and table, and the charming family. La Force, ever alert in desperate villany, was, like the adder of the old fable, scarcely warmed with the hospitality that sheltered and protected him, ere he sat down coolly to calculate the possibility of undermining and destroying for ever the peace and happiness of his benefactor: the ties of moral obligation would with La Force have weighed but little to prevent his insulting the virtue and modesty of De Tracy's wife and daughters; but in spite of his infamous passions, this diabolical intention readily gave way to a plan of a still blacker hue, of a more sweeping and comprehensive mischief.

The stay of De Tracy's family in the Bahamas being determined to be of several months, it was judged necessary to their convenience, as well as a prudent measure of security, to take with them the greatest part of the family plate, jewels, &c. as well as a considerable sum in specie to answer the calls of purchases and current expenses. On the forcible seizure of this treasure, the murder of its owner, and the brutal gratification of his hellish designs on his wife and daughters, to obtain these 'at one fell swoop,' it was that the insatiate demon La Force had set his mind!

The treasure was shipped under the gloating eye of La Force himself, and the unsuspecting victims being embarked, the Julie bore from these beloved scenes of his happiness, for ever, the ill-fated De Tracy. The vessel left the harbour amid the shouts of the assembled population of the estate, who shed tears of unaffected regret at their departure, and poured out prayers for their safety. A favourable light wind and smooth sea soon wafted the Julie from the multitude on the shore, and De Tracy, his wife, his children, his wealth, his all! were now in the hands and at the mercy of the ferocious La Force!

The confinement and sameness of a sea voyage were rendered less annoying to the family of De Tracy than they usually are, by the attentions of La Force; he joined in all their recreations, and afforded every facility to the indulgence of them. Much of the time was spent in conversation, in music, dancing, and in walking on deck enjoying the cool evening breezes; and when the dews of evening obliged them to descend to the cabin, the captain would entertain them with a relation of the various dangers which himself and other persons had encountered at sea, or detail, with an amusing gravity, some of the prevailing superstitions of sailors.

One delightfully clear morning, when they were in hourly expectation of making the land, La Force announced to De Tracy, that it was his intention to make that day a general festival, it being the anniversary of his birth. His orders were issued to the crew, and the ship's steward received his instructions to make the suitable arrangements for a day of rejoicing. La Force was jovial and apparently merry beyond his usual manner, and swallowed one cup of wine after another to the health and happiness of Madame De Tracy, her children, and her husband. In this elevation of spirits, he suddenly placed his hand on the arm of De Tracy, and said to him in an undervoice, 'My best friend, before we part, I have matters of the greatest importance to communicate to you; gratitude for the services you have rendered me, require that I should no longer conceal from you information which nearly concerns the welfare and happiness of your family.

I have for some time possessed papers of the utmost value, connected with your wife's property in this island; let me then, in some degree, discharge the debt of gratitude I owe, by explaining and placing them in your hands; let us retire for a few moments to my cabin, where, unobserved and undisturbed, we may examine them: follow me!'

The curiosity of De Tracy was strongly excited by this singular address, and he suffered La Force to conduct him below: when they arrived at the cabin, La Force opened the iron door of a small secret closet, formed among the larger timbers of the vessel, and beckoned him with a mysterious air to enter it. De Tracy's surprise was great; but expecting La Force to follow him, he did enter, and at the same instant felt the door shut upon him with a sudden violence, and heard La Force turning its massive lock on him on the outside. The astonished De Tracy heard the door of the outer cabin as quickly shut and locked, and the fiend, La Force, with loud laughter, bounding up the stairs upon deck; he remained a few moments, half-imagining the manoeuvre to be a jest; but he was now roused by the repeated shouts and peals of merriment among the crew, in which the voice of La Force could be distinguished. A feeling of dismay now began to force itself upon him, and a thousand little circumstances in the behaviour of La Force, unobserved before, flashed upon his mind at once.

In the midst of this increasing alarm, the voice of De Tracy's servant Dugald was now heard in loud tones of anger and reproach; the clashing of weapons succeeded, and the quick steps of the contending parties towards the cabin, and this was terminated by the sound of heavy blows and groans, as if of some one wounded in the conflict. The agitation and alarm of De Tracy rose to a dreadful pitch, when he was awakened to a full sense of his misery, by the sudden shriek after shriek of his beloved and lovely wife, and his daughters, uttered in all the piercing agony of anguish and despair! He was now totally undeceived; he entreated, he called, he prayed, he raved; in all the rage of infuriated madness, he used his utmost force; and though armed by anger and despair with almost supernatural might, the door, which opened inwards, withstood his utmost efforts. But why should we dwell minutely on a scene of such unutterable misery! What the unhappy man endured, and what were the sufferings of the woman he loved and adored, and the children he so dearly cherished, are fit only to be imagined, not surely to be spoken or written. But their wrongs were remembered, and their shrieks numbered by a POWER more potent and terrible than man, and a certain doom and deplorable death was pronounced against the guilty perpetrators of this horrid crime, at the moment when, in the height of their wickedness, they fancied their joy at the full.

The cries of affliction died away; the evening passed, and morning came. The all-glorious sun rose upon the foul and hellish deeds of the night; and through a crevice, which admitted light, the unhappy De Tracy found that his prison was, in fact, the treasure-room of a pirate vessel, for such he was convinced were these fiends in human shape: at the same moment a hole opened above, and a small portion of bread, and an antique silver cup, filled with water, were lowered down. Amidst the acute misery of his situation, it was but a light addition that De Tracy recognised the silver vessel to be part of the treasure, his own property, which he had shipped, and which, with the other valuable articles of the same description, was securely packed in strong chests, and which it was now evident were rifled. He could now measure the extent of his calamity, and with as much fortitude as he could gather, prepared himself for a fate, which, amongst such miscreants, could not be deemed far distant. *To be continued...*

The Sanguinary Life And Cruel Death Of A Robber

Thomas Dun was born in Bedfordshire, and even in child-hood, was noted for his pilfering propensity, and the cruelty of his disposition. He lived in the time of Henry I, and so many were his atrocities, that we can only find limits for the recital of a few.

His first exploit was on the highway to Bedford, where he met a wagon full of corn, going to market, drawn by a team of beautiful horses. He accosted the driver; and, in the middle of the conversation, stabbed him in the heart, with a dagger, which he always carried about his person. He buried the body, and mounting the wagon, proceeded to the town, where he sold all off, and decamped with the money. He continued to commit many petty thefts and assaults, but judging it safer to associate himself with others, he repaired to a gang of thieves, who infested the country leading from St Alban's to Tocester, where they became such a terror, that the king had to build a town to check his power in the country, and which retains his name to this day, namely Dunstable.

This precaution was however of little avail, for he pursued his courses to a great extent. Among the gang were many artists, who enabled him to pick locks, wrench bolts, and use deaf files with great effect. One day having heard that some lawyers were to dine at a certain inn in Bedford, about an hour before the appointed time, he came running to the inn, and desired the landlord to hurry the dinner, and to have enough ready for ten or twelve. The company soon arrived, and the lawyers thought Dun a servant of the house, while those of the house supposed him an attendant on the lawyers. He bustled about, and the bill being called for, he collected it; and having some change to return to the company, they waited till his return; but growing weary, they rang the bell, and enquired for their money, when they discovered him to be an impostor. With the assistance of his associates, he made clear off with a considerable booty of cloaks, hats, silver spoons, and every thing of value upon which he could lay his hands.

After this adventure, Dun and his associates went and put up at another inn. They rose in the night time, insulted the landlord, did violence to the landlady, then murdered them both, and pillaged the house of every thing valuable. Dun had an animosity to lawyers, and he determined to play a rich one a trick. He waited upon him, and very abruptly demanded payment of a bond which he had produced; and the gentleman found his name was so admirably forged, that he could not swear it was not his handwriting. He assured Dun, however, that he had never borrowed the money, and would not pay the bond. He then left him, assuring the lawyer that he would give him some employment. A law-suit was entered into, and several of his comrades came forward, and swore as to the debt being just, and he was about getting a decision in his favour, when the lawyer produced a forged receipt for the debt, which some of his clerks likewise swore to; upon which Dun was cast. He was in a great passion at being outwitted, and swore 'he never heard of such rogues, as to swear they paid him a sum which was never borrowed.'

This was one of the few instances where he did not display that barbarity of disposition which is evinced in all his other adventures, and which makes us refrain from the enumeration of many of them. He became, however, such a terror to every one, that the Sheriff of Bedford sent a considerable force to attack him in his retreat. Finding, upon a reconnoitre, however, that his force was equal, if not superior, to the Sheriff's, he commenced the attack, and completely routed them, taking eleven prisoners, whom he hung upon the trees round the wood, to scare others by the example of their fate. The clothes of those they had hanged, served to accomplish their next adventure, which was a design to rob the castle of a nobleman in the neighbourhood. They proceeded in the attire of the Sheriff's men, and demanded entrance in the name of the King, to make search for Dun. After searching every corner, they asked for the keys of the trunks to examine them, which when they received, they loaded themselves with booty, and departed. The nobleman complained to Parliament against the Sheriff, when, upon investigation, the trick was discovered.

Nothing prevented Dun from accomplishing any object which he had in view, as he possessed the greatest share of temerity and cruelty that could fall to the lot of a man. He would, under the disguise of a gentleman, wait upon rich people, and, upon being shewn into their room, murder them and carry away their money.

There was a rich knight in the neighbourhood, from whom Dun wished to have a little money. Accordingly he went and knocked at his door; the maid opening it, he enquired if her master was at home; and being answered in the affirmative, he instantly went up stairs, and familiarly entered his room. Common compliments having passed, he sat down in a chair, and began a humorous discourse, which attracted the attention of the knight. Dun then approached, and demanded a word or two in his ear: 'Sir,' says he, 'my necessities come pretty thick upon me at present, and I am obliged to keep even with my creditors, for fear of cracking my fame and fortune too. Now, having been directed to you by some of the heads of the parish, as a very considerable and liberal person, I am come to petition you in a modest manner to lend me a thousand marks, which will answer all the demand upon me at present!' 'A thousand marks!' answered the knight, 'why, man, that's a capital sum; and where's the inducement to lend you so much money, who are a perfect stranger to me; for my eyes and knowledge, I never saw you before all the days of my life!' – 'Sir, you must be mistaken, I am the honest grocer at Bedford, who has so often shared your favours.' 'Really, friend, I do not know you, nor shall I part with my money but on a good bottom: pray what security have you?' 'Why, this dagger,' says Dun, (pulling it out it of his breast) 'is my constant security; and unless you let me have a thousand marks instantly, I shall pierce your heart!' This terrible menace produced the intended effect, and he delivered the money.

By this time Dun had become formidable both to the rich and the poor; but one melancholy circumstance attended the depredations of this man, that almost in every instance, except those above narrated, they were stained with blood. He continued his infamous course above twenty years, the vicinity of the river Ouse in Yorkshire being the usual scene of his exploits; and being attended by fifty armed men on horseback, the inhabitants of the country were afraid to seize him.

Nor was his last adventure less remarkable than those of his former life. His infamy daily increasing, the people of

that district were determined no longer to suffer his depredations. Though Dun was informed of what was intended,
yet he still continued his wicked career. The country rising
at last against him, he and his gang were so closely pursued,
that they were constrained to divide, each taking shelter where he possibly could, and Dun concealed himself
in a small village; the general pursuit and search, however,
continuing, he was discovered, and the house he was in surrounded. Two of the strongest posted themselves at the door;
with irresistible courage Dun seized his dagger, laid them
both dead, bridled his horse, and in the midst of the uproar,
forced his way. To the number of a hundred and fifty, armed
with clubs, pitchforks, rakes, and whatever rustic weapons
they could find, pursued him, drove him from his horse, but
to the astonishment of all, he again mounted, and, with his
sword, cut his way through the crowd.

Multitudes flocking from all quarters, the pursuit was
renewed. He was, a second time, dismounted, and now
employed his feet: he ran for the space of two miles; but
when he halted to breathe a little, three hundred men were
ready to oppose him. His courage and strength, however,
still remaining unsubdued, he burst through them, fled over
a valley, threw off his clothes, seized his sword in his teeth,
and plunged into a river in order to gain the opposite bank.

To his sad surprise, however, he perceived it covered
with new opponents: he swam down the river, was pursued by several boats, until he took refuge on a small island.
Determined to give him no time to recover from his
fatigue, they attacked him there. Thus closely pursued, he
plunged again into the river with his sword in his teeth; he
was pursued by the boats, repeatedly struck with their oars;
and having received several strokes on the head, was at last
vanquished.

He was conducted to a surgeon to have his wounds
dressed, then led before a magistrate, who sent him to

Bedford jail under a strong guard. Remaining there two weeks, until he was considerably recovered, a scaffold was erected in the market place, and, without a formal trial, he was led forth to execution. When the two executioners approached him, he warned them of their danger if they should lay hands on him; he accordingly grasped both, and nine times overthrew them upon the stage before his strength was exhausted, so that they could not perform their duty. His hands were first chopped off at the wrist; then his arms at the elbow; next, about an inch from the shoulders; his feet below the ankles; his legs at the knee; and his thighs about five inches from his trunk; a horrible scene was closed by severing his head from the body, and consuming it to ashes; the other parts of his body were fixed up in the principle places of Bedfordshire, as a warning to his companions. The quantity of blood that was shed during his wicked career, restrains even the tear of pity upon his miserable fate.

Adventures of Morgan, Prince of Free-Booters: Torture and Horrors!

Continued from page 39…
Morgan continued at Maracäibo three weeks, and then advanced towards Gibraltar, whither he was persuaded all the opulent fugitives had fled. It was now three years since Olonois with his free-booters had appeared there. Peter the Picard, who accompanied him then, and who served as a guide to the present expedition, recollecting the bloody obstacles he had to surmount, prepared his comrades not to expect an easy victory. They were agreeably deceived. Some

resistance, indeed, was at first made; but the inhabitants shortly saved themselves by flight into the woods, where they intrenched themselves behind the trees.

Thus was Gibraltar a second time taken: that city which had been reduced to ashes by the freebooters, had been rebuilt since their departure, and again became the theatre of new horrors. The scenes so familiar to these covetous brigands, were again repeated: they hunted the fugitives, pillaged to a great distance, exercised tortures, and put in practice every horror that could dishonour victory. The pirates seemed now even to improve upon their accustomed ferocity: two hundred and fifty inhabitants were brought to them, chained and trembling. Never was their cruelty more terribly ingenious than in the inventions to which they resorted. Some of these wretched victims were fastened naked to crosses, and tortured with burning fire-brands; many others were hung up by their arms, while stones of a prodigious weight were attached to them, and consequently by this horrible extension the muscles were torn out from their sockets or fastenings, and the bones from their joints. There were some (shame and humility make one tremble with horror), who were suspended in a posture most disgusting, till their horribly mutilated bodies fell down from their own weight. In this manner, the unfortunate wretches languished four or five days under the most dreadful sufferings, unless some robber, from an impulse of compassion, terminated their woes by putting them to death.

The ever execrable authors of these atrocities exercised them indiscriminately on all their victims, whatever their age, condition, or colour might be. Women, decorated with all the graces of their sex.—children, who were protected by their innocence,—aged persons, whose weakness was their protection,—whites, mulattos, negroes,—all were involved in the same fate.

The slaves who betrayed their masters were for the most part rewarded with their liberty; though there were few who were willing to purchase it at that price. Some there were, who, out of revenge, wickedness, or inveterate hatred, denounced their masters, notwithstanding they had nothing to disclose. One of these false informations furnished the ferocious Morgan with an opportunity to disguise his cruelty under the mask of justice. A slave, who having denounced his master as being opulent, and who had thereby drawn upon him the most cruel tortures, was contradicted by the fact. For this atrocious falsehood the Spanish prisoners in a body demanded revenge: he was immediately abandoned by Morgan to the discretion of his master; who having refused that offer, and referred to that chieftain the care of pronouncing the wretch's fate, Morgan caused him to be instantly cut to pieces.

After six weeks' residence at Gibraltar, he demanded a ransom for the city, which he threatened to commit to the flames, and carried away several prisoners with him as hostages. Some of them who could not bear the idea of seeing their city, which had been so recently rebuilt, again become a heap of ruins, conjured him to allow them to go through the woods, that they might make an effort to raise the sums required. Morgan granted them a delay of eight days, commanding them to bring him the result of their inquiries at Maracäibo, whether he conducted their companions.

On his arrival at that city, he for the first time perhaps experienced a sensation of terror; nor could all the freebooters, who were in other respects so intrepid, dissemble their consternation. The first news they received was that three Spanish ships of war had already been dispatched in pursuit of them, and had already moored at the entrance of the lake. The fort of La Barra, which the pirates had deserted, had again been put into a state of defence. The largest vessel they had carried only fourteen small cannons; while one of the three Spanish men of war carried forty, another thirty-eight, and the other twenty-four pieces of cannon. To escape such superior force was utterly impossible: for the Spaniards had so disposed themselves, as to leave only a narrow and very dangerous passage between the ships of war on one side, and the fort on the other, by which the freebooters could not go out. These robbers considered themselves lost without resource: Morgan alone, who soon recovered himself from his first terror, still retained some hope, and displayed his usual courage.

His first operation was to send out one of his ships to the mouth of the river, to acquire exact information as to the position of the Spaniards, as well as concerning the number and strength of their ships. The reports which were in consequence made to him were not the most consolatory. They confirmed the first news, with this addition,– that the Spanish crews were very considerable, and were labouring with great activity to repair the fort, on which their flag was hoisted. However embarrassing this situation was, Morgan thought that, in order to maintain the character of the freebooters, he ought to oppose a bravado to such imminent danger. He therefore sent one of his prisoners to the Spanish admiral, to demand twenty thousand piasters for the ransom of Maracäibo, which was in his possession. In case of a refusal, he should proceed to burn that city and cut all his prisoners to pieces.

Such unexpected insolence disconcerted the Spaniards; whose commander, Don Alphonso del Campo y Espinola, sent him a formal answer, in which he frankly told Morgan that he had been sent to chastise the freebooters;– that the moment was now arrived when he (Morgan) saw it was impossible for him to escape with his fleet, – that nevertheless, if he would restore all the plunder he had taken, both in gold, silver, jewels, and merchandise, and would surrender up all his prisoners, including the slaves, he would allow him to retire peaceably; but that, in case of a refusal, all the freebooters should be exterminated; and that his fate was so much the more inevitable, as his brave soldiers were desirous of nothing more than to avenge the cruelties which the corsairs had inflicted on their countrymen. With regard to the article of ransom, Don Alphonso verbally replied as follows, by means of the messenger: 'Tell Morgan, that I will pay him the ransom he demands only with shot; and that I charge myself with the bringing of that kind of currency.'

Such an answer had been expected by Morgan, who had formed his determination in consequence. As soon as the messenger returned, he convened his comrades in the square of Maracäibo, to whom he communicated the commander's letter and verbal reply, and then asked them,– 'Will you purchase your liberty by the sacrifice of all your plunder? Or would you rather fight in defence of it?' They all unanimously declared that they would fight to the very last drop of their blood, rather than give up, in such a cowardly manner, what had cost them so many dangers. But when they had reflected fasting upon their situation, and had coolly compared their strength with the forces of their adversaries, this effusion of enthusiasm subsided a little. Never before had any company or body of freebooters been placed in such critical circumstances, in which their courage was paralysed, and in which they could neither foresee nor expect a favourable conclusion. On the following day, therefore, they authorized their captain to submit these proposals to the Spanish admiral:– 'The freebooters offer to evacuate the Maracäibo, without committing any damage to the city, and without insisting further on the ransom; and at the same time to set at liberty all the prisoners, half the slaves, and the hostages they had brought from Gibraltar as securities for the contributions promised.'

These proposals were contemptuously rejected by Don Alphonso, who left the pirates only two days to accept his first capitulation. If they persisted in refusing it, they should experience all his power: it only remained for the pirates to make their choice between a shameful retreat, preceded by the restitution of all their booty, and a mortal engagement.

From this moment Morgan excited all his brave companions in arms to the most persevering activity. He ordered all his hostages, prisoners, and slaves to be secured, and carefully watched: next he ordered all the pitch, tar, and sulphur he had, to be collected together, as well as all the gunpowder he could spare, in order to convert one of his largest vessels into a fire-ship; whither he directed all his combustibles to be conveyed. He formed various masses of pitch and sulphur, mixed with tar and powder, and proper to be shot; and took every possible measure to give the greatest effect to these extraordinary expedients. The side planks of the ships were prepared on the inside in such a manner that they would burst and shiver to pieces: there was not a single stratagem that he did not conceive, in order to conceal both the nature and extent of his defensive resources. Upon deck were placed blocks of wood dressed like men, with hats, arms, and coloured clothes; so that these figures might at a distance be taken for soldiers. In the body of the vessel were made several port holes, in which were placed pieces of painted wood, rounded in the shape of cannons. On her helm was hoisted a large English flag, that nothing might even seem to be wanting, in order to give her the appearance of a large English ship of war. This vessel was to open the way, and the other barks of various sizes were to follow her in a line one after the other. In one of them were contained all the male prisoners; in another were all the women, together with all the valuable effects, consisting of silver and diamonds; while the remainder of the plunder was distributed on board the other ships. But previously to setting sail, every freebooter was obliged to swear, between Morgan's hands, that they would fight without asking quarter, until their very last gasp.

The Spanish admiral had allowed them only two days for reflection, at the expiration of which he was to attack them. That period had elapsed, and he had not appeared; nor, indeed, had they heard any thing spoken concerning him. In fact, the Spaniards had so calculated on the superiority of their force, that all precipitation on their part seemed unnecessary. They did not consider that these men, who were so formidable in their operations, would find in despair an increase of energy. In short, the Spaniards, blinded by conceit, disdained to observe, that with such men they had not an hour to lose; and thus left Morgan the time that was necessary to complete his preparations for a most desperate attack.

To be continued…

Assassination Of Count Jacucco

In 1818, while the King of Naples and Cardinal Gonsalvi were occupied at Rome in giving sumptuous feasts, the *Campagna* of Rome and the mountains were infested with a great number of Brigands, who devastated the country, and committed the most atrocious crimes.

… The bandit De Cessaris was at that time committing great atrocities in the vicinity of Amigri and Frosinone. Among other barbarities which he committed, the following is enough to make one shudder with horror; Count Jacucco, of Anagri, was going one day with his two daughters, on foot, through his grounds, one mile distant from the town of Anagri, when he was surprised by De Cessaris and ten of his band. The count and his two daughters were seized, they were forbidden to speak, and the robber

demanded 10,000 crowns of them as their ransom. The Count replied that he consented to this demand, but that it was necessary to write home, as he did not carry such a sum about him. 'Very well,' said Cessaris, 'come with me to the mountains, and write from thence, and we will allow you to go when we get the money.' The poor count was very corpulent, and could not walk, as the assassins said, and they were afraid of a surprise, being so close to the town. In fact, the gen-d'armerie of Anagri had received intimation of the approach of the Brigands, and were making preparations to pursue them, without having much hope of rescuing the captured family. The Brigands hearing of this pursuit, and the count not being able to walk, they killed him on the spot before the eyes of his daughters; he fell under seven or eight strokes of the stiletto. The assassins then took the girls on their shoulders, who seeing their father thus sacrificed, and themselves in the arms of the Brigands, became so dreadfully alarmed, that one of them lost her reason. The gendarmes following the traces of the Brigands, found the count still alive, but who died a few moments afterwards.

The pursuit of the gendarmes continued, but was quite fruitless, as they never overtook the assassins. At the end of two days, letters came from the two girls to their uncle, requiring that 10,000 crowns should immediately be sent, when from thirty to forty persons were to be liberated, who were detained like themselves. The uncle sent the desired sum, and at the end of five days, during which time they were detained for the amusement of the robbers, the two girls were released. They could give no account of where they had been, as they were conducted blindfold to the bottom of the mountains, where they found provisions, which the robbers took on their mules, and then conducted them, almost dead, to their home.

Since then, De Cessaris has continued his crimes.

Piracy, Murder And Rape: Part Two

Continued from page 47…
The morning was not far advanced, when the sun dipped at once into a dark and tempestuous ocean of clouds; the wind began to whistle loudly through the rigging; and the prisoner could now clearly perceive that the weather was threatening, when he felt a flurried motion of the ship, and heard a voice, which he knew to be La Force's, in the broken and feeble accents of intoxication, call 'Put her before the wind, and let her go where she pleases.' It now became evident, from the rushing of the water, that the velocity of the ship's progress was tremendously increased; and it was equally evident, that

there was a general incapacity of the crew to manage her. The wind now blew very fresh, and the ship went through the water at a rate of ten miles an hour. The night looked dreary and turbulent: the sky was covered with large fleeces of broken clouds, and the stars flashed angrily through them, as they were wildly hurried along by the blast. The sea began to run high, and the masts showed, by their incessant creaking, that they carried more sail than they could well contain.

… De Tracy lay in speechless agony and utter despair; the noise and confusion on deck every moment increased; and, while musing on the probability of being dispatched by these villains, infuriated by drunkenness as they now were, to his astonishment he heard himself accosted by name, and in friendly language, by his faithful Dugald. 'My loved and injured master, put your trust in Him whose power can still the tempest, THE HOUR IS COME!' In a moment the lock was turned, and the door opened; the same faithful voice said, 'Take this sword, and follow me in silence; if you have the courage to avenge the unutterable miseries and death of your beautiful and wretched wife and daughters, come, for the hour is at hand, and by the help of the Almighty, who protects you, and will avenge your wrongs, I will support you.' The unhappy husband followed with a resolved step and in silence, as he was bid.

They came on deck, where, by the gleam of a torch nailed against the mast, and the quick succession of lightning, which now flashed fiercely and rapidly, Dugald silently pointed to a scene which the hope of sure and immediate revenge rendered inexpressibly sweet. The infamous La Force and ten sailors, though nearly overcome with wine, were seated on deck: the remainder of the crew had been conveyed below in a state of complete intoxication and insensibility. The scene might be conceived to resemble the revelry of evil spirits in their infernal regions; some shouted, some sang, and they blasphemed the Being whose all-seeing eye even now rested on them in its anger; one loud din of cursing and carousal echoed far and wide: the mingled clamours which ascended from this scene of wickedness and debauchery partook of all the evil qualities of debased minds, and the most infamous pursuits, and cannot be described. Discord and confusion had their full share in the tumultuous conference between La Force and his diabolical confederates, who were vociferously debating on the share they were respectively to enjoy of the plunder and destruction of the miserable De Tracy and his family. Louder and louder grew the horrid clamour of blood; recriminations followed, with boasting declarations of the part each had taken in the horrible transaction of the previous night; the nature and extent of his injury was thus fully developed to the agonised De Tracy. The drunken ruffians soon came to blows amongst themselves; they drew their weapons generally; and ill-directed blows and ineffectual stabs were given and received in the flashing and unsteady light.

De Tracy, gliding like a spectre amongst them, thrust one of them through and through; a second, a third, and a fourth dropped from his sword, ere they saw who was amongst them; in the mean time Dugald's arm had been faithful, and three of the wretched miscreants had fallen beneath his trusty weapon. La Force, on the first recognition of De Tracy, and Dugald fighting at his side, leaped upon an arm chest, and discharged his pistols. De Tracy and Dugald, with one impulse, but still in deadly silence, sprang upon him, and in a few moments he was also stretched among the slain. Three yet remained unhurt; but dispirited by their loss, and terrified at the unexpected visitation, they were quickly lying with their infamous companions.

De Tracy and Dugald now barricaded the gangway, and secured the cabin and the hatches; and after returning thanks to God for his merciful interposition, De Tracy, with a fainting and a heavy heart, inquired of his faithful servant for his wife and children! The honest and affectionate heart of Dugald melted as he gave the narrative. The convulsive sobs and groans of the wretched husband audibly told his agony and distress, and seemed to threaten the termination of his own existence. Of the brutal dishonour of his wife and daughters, he was already too well informed; but he had yet to be told their ultimate fate. His tortured brain had yet to learn, that his youngest daughter had not survived the horrible treatment she had received; that his eldest son had, in youthful indignation, lifted a weapon against La Force in his mother's defence, and had been literally hewn to pieces by the barbarian before her eyes! That his wife, with his youngest son and the infant, had been forced into a small canoe with his mulatto servant, and set adrift during the height of the gale; and that at the moment of their departure, his eldest daughter, in a state of exhaustion and insensibility, had been thrown into the sea to her raving mother, in mockery of her cries for her remaining child, and had there perished, in her sight! The possibility of a slight and crazy boat out-living the hurricane of the preceding night was all the hope that remained to the unhappy De Tracy of the wretched remnant of his family.

As dawn approached, the storm increased in violence; the gale roared through the rigging; and the sea, upturned by sudden and heavy gusts of wind, showed, as far as the eye could see, the dark and tremendous furrows so fatal to the mariner. Heavy billows now rolled around the ship, nearly as high as her mast-head, and now flashed and swept over the deck; the vessel hurried onwards with a terrific rapidity; her seams admitted water, and on every side symptoms manifested themselves of her speedy destruction; the only chance of safety lay in standing out to sea, by keeping the ship before the wind; and Dugald, with that view, determined to lash himself to the helm. In this attempt, a sudden lurch of the vessel shifted the rudder violently, and he was laid prostrate and senseless on the deck, by a blow from the tiller, and De Tracy hastened to his assistance.

At this moment a figure, that crouched amongst the slain, and seemed one of their number, started on its feet before the astonished De Tracy, vigorous and unhurt; it was La Force, who had escaped his fate from the swords of De Tracy and Dugald, by a breast-plate of mail, which he wore beneath his clothes, as a measure of precaution against the treachery of his own crew; and who, to avoid a personal encounter with two determined men, had sunk, unhurt, among his companions at their first attack. Before De Tracy had recovered himself from the surprise at his appearance, the miscreant had fired a pistol-shot, which, unhappily, took effect in his right shoulder, and before he could either grapple with his murderous opponent, or take any measures for farther defence, La Force had completed his monstrous career of evil, and the broken-hearted De Tracy was released from his earthly suffering which oppressed him. The unhappy man received the dagger of La Force in his chest, and he was mercifully spared pangs of recollection: his death was instantaneous.

Dugald, from the effects of his blow, was still insensible to all that passed; and La Force experienced no opposition to all his measures. He instantly attached one or two cannon shot to the corpse of the unhappy man, and unrelentingly consigned it to the devouring deep. He proceeded to secure Dugald, before his recovery from his accident should render it difficult or impossible. He dragged him to the mast, to which, ere his senses had returned, he found himself bound hand-and-foot. The exulting fiend now seemed to have overcome all obstacle to the full completion of his crime, and wanted but the assistance of his fellows, who were still fastened below, totally incapable of any exertion.

Through the thickness of the storm, Dugald now fancied he saw a small boat dancing on the tremendous waves at a short distance to leeward of the ship; now buried in the trough of the sea, and lost to his straining sight for some moments; now quivering between life and death on the raging summit of a billow, and again shooting down its roaring declivity, as if to destruction. The ship continued to gain on the frail bark, and, to the hopes and imagination of Dugald, it seemed to enjoy a special protection; for he could now perceive that it contained the precious burden of his beloved mistress and her remaining children, and he could distinctly observe the mulatto throwing up her arms in signal to the ship.

Through the gleaming openings of the disturbed elements, there now appeared, about two miles from the starboard bow, a large ship, scudding before the wind, suffering, like themselves, under the storm, but evidently in good condition. The haunted imagination of La Force now saw before him the choice of punishment, a dreadful death with his devoted companions with the sinking vessel, or an ignominious and public punishment by the intervention of the passing ship. The evidence of Dugald would, in that case, be conclusive against him, and the wretched criminal yet conceived the thought of embruing his guilty hands in his blood also: but his doom was fixed. The remaining mast, to which Dugald was confined, was at this moment carried away by a heavy shock, and in the wreck of its fall he was so far released as to be able to disengage himself entirely.

La Force, who, in his distraction, had not observed the canoe towards which the ship was driving, was now springing forward to an attack on Dugald; Dugald, on his part, had seized a crow-bar as a weapon, and, meeting the enraged monster in his advance, placed himself in a position of defence, and pointed out to his astonished sight the canoe in which four of his victims were thus miraculously preserved, and the floating corpse of the murdered De Tracy, which, from its natural buoyancy, and the shifting of the ballast, by which it was sunk, to the feet, now swam erect in the water, exposed below the breast, and had drifted towards the vessel, as if seeking judgement on its destroyer. The inanimate body seemed to the staring eye-balls of La Force to be the visitation of a spirit; the villain was nerveless; he raved for mercy, attempted prayer, and called, in vain, on his companions for succour; at this moment the ship, which had been for some time but struggling with her fate, made a lurch, which threw her broadside to the sweeping sea; she instantly filled, and shot down head-foremost. Dugald sprang from the stern in time to avoid the whirlpool of the sinking ship. La Force, in an attempt to throw himself over-board, was entangled by the head in the fallen rigging, and on his knees, screaming for mercy was the blood-stained and despairing wretch literally dragged, half strangled to the bottom, with the vessel.

Dugald reached the canoe in safety, and succeeded in keeping it afloat till they were perceived by a passing ship, and rescued from their impending destruction.

The youngest son, who had been forced into the canoe with the unhappy mother, died from the severity of the exposure, adding a fifth victim to the monster, La Force! Madame De Tracy, with her infant, and the mulatto, Rachel, were, with considerable difficulty, recovered from the effects of their brutal treatment, and were ultimately enabled to reach the scenes of their former happiness.

Adventures of Morgan, Prince of Freebooters: Attack Of The Fire-Ship

Continued from page 59…

At the end of six days he was ready; and, on the 29th April, 1669, he advanced toward the Spaniards, who were quietly at anchor. The dawn was just beginning to appear. The admiral, whose ship was moored in the channel, expeditiously prepared to receive the enemy; and mistaking the fire-ship for the chief of the pirates' vessels, he suffered it to approach him. He was astonished that, although it was so near, and had such a numerous crew upon deck, not a single cannon was fired. Supposing the freebooter intended to board him (as he knew it was their favourite manoeuvre) he suspended his firing, in order that he might oppose the stronger resistance. Nothing could render the pirates a greater service than this inactivity: never was the truth of the ancient proverb more verified, that 'fortune favours the bold.'

A few well-directed cannon-shots were sufficient to shatter the frail machine to pieces, and sink it to the bottom; as, in fact, it was scarcely the skeleton of a vessel. The Spaniards did not perceive this error until the fire-ship was close by them: from that moment all their efforts to stop its progress were useless. The few freebooters on board, fastened it to a Spanish ship, and, as is usual in this kind of operations, rapidly threw themselves into a canoes which had been brought for that purpose. The Spanish admiral, however, displayed much presence of mind: he ordered several Spaniards to board the fire-ship, in order to cut down its masts, and, if it were possible, to prevent the explosion; but his active adversaries were beforehand with him, and, as they were quitting the fire-ship, had already kindled the combustibles it contained. In a very short time the admiral's ship took fire, which raged with such vehemence, that she was almost instantly buried in the waves, together with the greater part of the crew. Many of the Spaniards had thrown themselves into the sea, and were endeavouring to save themselves by swimming, but they sank before they could reach the shore. Some of them indeed might have received assistance from the freebooters, who, from motives of humanity, or some other impulse more congenial to their character endeavoured to rescue them from the sea; but the Spaniards preferred perishing, rather than owe their lives to these ferocious enemies, from whom they apprehended a treatment worse, perhaps, than death. A very small number only succeeded in landing; among whom was the Spanish admiral, who had taken refuge in a shallop, the moment he saw his ship in flames.

The freebooters availed themselves of their first moment of the enemies' consternation, to attack the second ship of war: which they took by boarding, after a slight resistance. They made the air re-echo with their cries of victory, as soon as they beheld the principal vessel disappear. At the sight of these astonishing events which to them seemed miraculous, the Spaniards on board the third ship were struck with such a panic, that they thought less of fighting than of saving themselves. They therefore cut their cables, and rapidly made for the fort; before which they bored their vessel, and sunk her to the bottom. The pirates hastened to seize at least a few pieces of the floating wreck; but the moment the Spaniards that were on shore saw them approaching, they set the wreck on fire.– All these circumstances, just related, occupied no more than one hour.

This astonishing deliverance at so critical an emergency, and the gaining of such a signal and complete victory in so short a time, with such little force, and without losing a single man, was to the pirates almost a dream. But they were not content with it: they determined without delay to attack the fort, which was guarded by the seamen who had saved themselves, not indeed with the hope of finding any thing to plunder, but merely that they might impress the Spaniards with an exalted idea of their courage. The Spaniards, however, had to congratulate themselves on their foresight in putting the fort into a state of defence: under the conduct of the admiral, who had likewise fled thither, they made such excellent use of their cannons, and in general defended themselves with so much vigour, that the pirates, who could neither raise batteries, nor plant ladder against the walls, were obliged to relinquish the attack, and withdrew on board their ships somewhat confused, and bitterly regretted their folly, having lost thirty men killed, and forty wounded.

From a Spanish pilot, who fell into their hands, Morgan received explanation of all that had occurred previous to their arrival. The hostile fleet, which was at first six ships strong, had been sent out from Spain for the express purpose of exterminating the freebooters; but the two largest vessels, each of which was mounted with thirty-six guns, were thought incapable of being effectively employed in the American latitudes; they were therefore sent back, and one of them was sunk in a storm. Don Alphonso, whose chief ship (the St Louis) was manned by a crew of three hundred men, was dispatched with the rest of the squadron in quest of the freebooters. Not meeting with them, either at Hispaniola, Campechy, St Domingo, or Caracas, he congratulated himself on finding them at Maracäibo. Two days before the fatal catastrophe, he was informed by a negro, who had escaped from the pirates, that they were preparing a fire-ship: he received this news with disdain.– 'How can those rascals,' said he, 'have ingenuity enough to construct such a ship? Where will they find the instruments and materials necessary for the purpose?' The Spanish pilot also related that on board the vessel which had been sunk there was silver, both in bullion and money, to the value of thirty thousand piasters.

This information Morgan thought ought not to be neglected; and his active freebooters spared no pains to draw up this treasure from the sea; and thus pay themselves for so many fatigues, from which they had hitherto gained nothing but glory. Morgan therefore left one ship behind, the crew of which succeeded in dragging up from the bottom of the sea about twenty quintals, as well in ingots as in moveables, both in silver and piasters. This interval was employed by that indefatigable commander in returning to Maracäibo with the remainder of his fleet. He there appropriated to his own use the frigate that had been captured from the Spaniards, and which mounted twenty-four guns, being the smallest vessel of their squadron. He repeated his injunction to the Spanish admiral of paying a ransom for the town, if he was desirous of rescuing it from total destruction: but the latter, overwhelmed with the weight of his misfortunes, insensible to any other losses than those he had already experienced, and having nothing to apprehend for himself from the destruction with which Maracäibo was threatened, would listen to no such proposition. But the terrified inhabitants were more tractable: without the admiral's permission, they capitulated with Morgan, and gave him twenty thousand piasters, by way of ransom, and five hundred head of cattle for the sustenance of his crew.

Still, however, the freebooters had another great difficulty to surmount. In order to re-enter the ocean from the lake, they had to pass close under that fort which had resisted their valour, and had cost them so many men; to have attempted a second attack would have been imprudent; as its success was, at the very best, very uncertain, and, even if they were successful, it would not increase their booty. On the other hand, if they risked a passage under the cannons of that formidable fort, their ships would either be dismantled or at least greatly damaged; and the majority, if not all, of themselves, being incapable of pursuing their route, would fall into the hands of their enemies. In this dilemma, Morgan tried what effect the boldness of his language and new threats would produce: he therefore sent a message to Don Alphonso, to inform him, that he would set all prisoners at liberty, provided a free passage was granted; but that, in the case of a refusal, he would hang them up upon the masts of the ships; and that, notwithstanding, he pledged his word to the Spaniards that he would pass in defiance of every obstacle.

Some prisoners were charged with the conveyance of this severe message to the admiral, whom they conjured with tears to take pity on their wives and children: but the Spanish admiral was inexorable; he was too much chagrined in having lost his fleet in such a manner; he still flattered himself that he might be able to repair his disgrace, and alleviate his vexation, by precipitating those insolent pirates to the bottom of the sea, at the very moment they were passing. The persons deputed by Morgan, who were so exceedingly interested in the success of the mission, interceding for their friends, for their families, and for themselves, met therefore with a very different reception. The admiral reproached them with their cowardice, and told them,– 'If you had prevented the entrance of these pirates, as I am determined to prevent their departure, you would never have been in your present situation.'

They had no other answer to carry back; and Morgan received the admiral's reply with his usual arrogance. 'Well then,' said he, 'since the admiral persists in refusing me free passage, I will find a way by which to pass, without his consent,' and took his measures accordingly.

First, he ordered every one to take the plunder he had collected, in order that it might be immediately divided among the freebooters. It was estimated at two hundred and fifty thousand piasters, in gold, silver, and precious stones, without reckoning the slaves and an immense quantity of merchandise. Every individual then received his share, which he was from that moment charged to defend.

While the division was carrying into effect, Morgan conceived a military manoeuvre. Early in the morning he caused some hundreds of freebooters to be conducted in small vessels and canoes, and to be landed in a place abounding with tall reeds. After lying concealed there for some hours, they returned one by one to their canoes, creeping closely along the ground, walking partly on their hands, and in short adopting every possible precaution to prevent discovery. Having thus reached their canoes, they lay down on board, either flat on their back or with their face downwards; and the canoes, which to all appearances were empty, were rowed back to the spot they had quitted. This manoeuvre was repeated several times during the course of the day, even in sight of the fort; so as to persuade the Spaniards that all the freebooters were disembarked, and that they would not fail to attack them during the following night.

Deceived by these appearances, the Spaniards stationed all their large guns on that side, and likewise posted nearly the whole of their soldiers there, so as to leave the side next to the sea almost in a defenceless state. This was precisely what the freebooters had calculated upon; and they availed themselves of this circumstance with their accustomed address. On the approach of night, they all went on board the ships, raised their anchors during the night, and abandoning themselves to the current, they did not unfurl their sails until they were actually in front of the fort. The light of the moon disclosed to the Spaniards, though somewhat too late, their enemies' stratagem. They hastily reconducted their cannons to the side near the sea, and commenced a very sharp fire, but which produced scarcely any effect. The course of the pirates was favoured by the wind: their ships sustained only trifling damages; and they successfully reached the ocean, after having taken leave of the fort by several discharges of artillery. The moment Morgan was out of danger, he landed all his prisoners on the adjacent shore, except the hostages he carried away from Gibraltar, as the ransom of that place had not been completely discharged. *To be continued...*

Mistaken Remorse

Simon Brown, the dissenting clergyman, exhibited a striking instance of the operation of remorse upon wounded sensibility. Brown fancied he had been deprived by the Almighty of his immortal soul, in consequence of having accidentally taken away the life of the highwayman, although it was done in the act of resistance to his threatened violence, and in protection of his own person. Whilst kneeling upon the wretch whom he succeeded in throwing upon the ground, he suddenly discovered that his prostrate enemy was deprived of life. This unexpected circumstance produced so violent an impression upon his nervous system, that he was overpowered by the idea of even involuntary homicide; and, for this imaginary crime, fancied himself ever after to be condemned to one of the most dreadful punishments that could be inflicted upon a human being.

The singular imagination of Brown was that for this involuntary crime, his soul had deserted his body, the latter being allowed to exist in that wretched state as an awful warning. Under the influence of this malady, Brown sent to Queen Caroline, the consort of George the Second, a book written with great acuteness, accompanied by a letter, the conclusion of which alludes to himself as a monument of divine wrath in the loss of his soul.

Ruse-De-Guerre

The fatal duel between the Duke of Hamilton and Lord Mohun, is well known. Macartney, the second to Lord Mohun, was suspected of having stabbed the duke treacherously; a reward was offered for apprehending him. About that time, a gentleman was set upon by highwaymen, and with a happy presence of mind, told them he was Macartney. On this, they brought him to a justice of the peace, in hopes of a reward, when he gave charge against them for robbery, and they were sent to jail.

Socivizca, The Morlachian Robber

A man named Socivizca was endeavouring to recover his wife and child, who had been seized by the Turks. His attempts by fair means were fruitless, and he resolved to resume his former occupation [of public robber and murderer of the Turks], and to avenge himself on the bashaw's subjects. For this purpose he put himself at the head of twenty-five companions, all of them intrepid, and in the vigour of youth. With this chosen band he took the road for Serraglio, the first Turkish town beyond the Venetian frontiers: for he had the prudence not to commit any act of violence within the Venetian state, that he might not make that government responsible for his depredations.

In a few days he met with a Turkish caravan, consisting of one hundred horses, laden with rich merchandise, escorted by seventy men. The Turks seeing him accompanied by so strong a band, though they were so much superior, dreaded him to such a degree, that they fled with the utmost precipitation, and only one merchant lost his life in defence of his valuable effects. This audacious robbery alarmed the whole Ottoman empire. Parties were sent out against him from all quarters; he was sought for in the mountains, and in the valleys; every field, and almost every bush, was beat, as if they had been in chace of a wild boar: but this was all mockery to disguise their cowardice; for while all these parties were making such strict researches, he and his companions appeared at noon-day in their villages, and supplied themselves with provisions in the markets of their towns.

He generally lodged his booty at a convent of Caloyers, an order of friars of the Greek church, who make a vow of rigid abstinence, but whose religion does not prevent them harbouring the Aiduzee (highwaymen) of the country, and sharing their plunder: the guardian of one of these convents, situated at Dragovich, seven miles beyond the springs of Cettina, was his particular friend; and here he often retired, separating himself from his companions for many months, so that the Turks often thought he was dead; while he was waiting only for an opportunity to fall upon them, and to exterminate as many of their race as possible. At length his robberies and massacres became insupportable to the Ottomans, and occasioned great inconveniences to the Venetian state; for they were the constant source of quarrels between the inhabitants of the frontiers of the two powers, so that it became the interest of the latter to seize him; therefore, upon every new complaint of the Turks, the government of Dalmatia increased the reward offered to take him, dead or alive.

Socivizca was not insensible of the great danger he was in of being seized by open force, or betrayed by some false friend, for the sake of the price set on his head; yet such is the force of habit, that nothing could deter him from continuing his depredations against the Turks. In the course of the year 1760, a certain Turk, whose name Acia Smaich, a very formidable man in the opinion of his countrymen, and in his own idea a great hero, boasted in all companies, that Socivizca durst not encounter him in single combat. It happened, however, that this man, and one of his brothers, escorted, with eight others, a rich caravan, which passed through a village near Glamoz, in the Ottoman territories, where Socivizca, and six of his comrades, lay concealed, waiting for an opportunity to exercise their valour, and to gain some considerable booty. By their spies they easily got intelligence who was at the head of the escort; and Socivizca, who was not of a temper to put up with the insolence of Smaich, went out to meet the caravan, and as soon as he approached it, publicly called upon the Turk to defend himself. Smaich advancing, instantly fired his carbine at Socivizca; and aimed so well, that the ball grazed the upper part of his head: fortunately for him, he had turned himself, to see that the enemy did not surround him while he was engaged with his adversary, and in this position the ball passed obliquely, and only gave him a slight wound; but it rendered him desperate, and with amazing rapidity he fired his carbine, and with a second shot, killed Smaich on the spot. His companions instantly fled; but five of them were overtaken in the pursuit, and put to death by Socivizca's companions.

After they had plundered the caravan, and divided the spoils, they disguised themselves, and took different roads, the better to avoid the researches of the Turks, who generally go in search of troops of robbers, and pay little attention to single persons on the road. For some time after this event, Socivizca lived so quiet and retired, that it was generally believed he was dead; but when it was least expected, he suddenly appeared again, at the head of a formidable banditti, consisting of twenty-five stout young men, with whom he marched to attack a very considerable caravan, that was going from Ragusa into Turkey, with a prodigious quantity of visclini, a silver coin of base alloy, worth about fourpence of our money. At the first onset, they killed seventeen of the Turks, and took three prisoners; which so terrified the rest of the guards, that they fled with the utmost precipitation, and left him in quiet possession of the treasure.

Socivizca was no sooner arrived at a neighbouring wood, than he ordered two of his prisoners to be impaled alive, and assigned to the third, the dreadful office of turning the stake, which was passed through their bodies, before a slow fire. His companions advised him to put the third to death; but, instead of this, when the two victims were half roasted, he ordered their heads to be cut off, which he delivered to the surviving prisoner with this commission: 'Carry those to the bashaw of Trawnick, and tell him from me, that if he does not release my wife and children, without delay, I will serve every Turk who falls into my hands in the same manner; and God only knows what excessive pleasure it would give me to roast the bashaw himself!'

Adventures of Morgan, Prince of Free-Booters: A Terrible Storm!

Continued from page 73...

Scarcely had his ship regained the ocean, when they encountered a horrible tempest, which threatened them with a loss which appeared the most inevitable as they were all more or less damaged. The pirates lost their anchors and their masts, and were also in momentary apprehension of being sunk: the wind tossed them about with incessant violence. On the one hand they were contiguous to a coast where they could not land without risking great dangers of another description; behind them were the Spaniards who would have gladly availed themselves of such an opportunity of retaliation. Never were navigators placed in a more critical situation. Some of their ships admitted water from every side, notwithstanding the indefatigable exertions made by the crews to keep the pumps going, beside the other expedients usually resorted to in such cases. Others were so much shattered by the storm that it became necessary to bind them together in various parts with thick cables, to prevent their falling to pieces. This hurricane, which was accompanied with thunder and lightning, continued four days without intermission: and, during the whole of that period, the freebooters' eyes were (to use one of the pirates' expressions) constantly open for fear they should be shut for ever. When calm weather was restored, alarms succeeded, which were not less acute than those they had already experienced, though of another kind. They discovered six ships, which at first they took, in the moment of despair, to be Spaniards; but their fear was quickly converted into joy. The ships were a French squadron under the command of admiral D'Estrees, from whom they received that assistance of which they stood in such pressing need. For the present, therefore, the pirates separated, some of them sailing for St Domingo, while the rest, who were under the command of Morgan, directed their course to Jamaica, where they arrived without encountering further accidents.

Morgan had, from his various expedients, acquired an immense fortune; and was at length desirous of enjoying some repose; but his comrades speedily dissipated the produce of their depredations, and had even contracted new debts. They besought him, therefore, to plan new enterprises, in such a pressing manner, that he yielded to their entreaties. The moment his resolution was taken and known, the free-booters flocked together from all parts, from Jamaica, St Domingo, and Tortuga; some in ships, others in canoes, in order to place themselves under his command. This example was followed by a great number of hunters from the island of St Domingo, who had never been on the sea, and who crossed vast forests, that they might join him.

The 24th day of October, 1670, was fixed upon for their departure...

At length the fleet under his orders, the greatest that had been commanded by a free-booter in the West Indian seas, was ready to set sail. It consisted of thirty-seven ships, of various rates; the admiral's ship carrying thirty-two, the others twenty, eighteen, and seventeen pieces of cannon; and the smallest four pieces. On board the fleet there was a great quantity of ammunition, together with powder machines of a new invention, and also two hundred marines, exclusive of the seamen and swabbers.

With such force great expectations might be formed: Morgan, therefore, promised his free-booters that, on their return, they should have wherewith to spend their days agreeably; provided, as already had too often happened, they did not attack places of little strength, but would direct their valour against the strongest; for experience had caused

Morgan to adopt this principle:— Where the Spaniards obstinately defend themselves, there is something to take; consequently their best fortified places are those which contain most treasure.

Morgan hoisted on his main-mast the royal flag of England, and divided his naval forces into two squadrons, distinguished by red and white flags, and formally assumed the title of admiral. He afterwards nominated a vice-admiral for each squadron, who took an oath of fidelity to him; established signals; and chose all his officers... Morgan also formally issued patents and letters of marque, empowering them to attack with hostilities, and in every possible manner, the Spaniards, both on land and sea, so long as they were the declared enemies of his sovereign, the king of England.

After these acts of authority, Morgan assembled all his officers, on whom he conferred full powers to sign in the name of the whole fleet, a convention or agreement with regard to plunder. It was stipulated that Morgan, as admiral, should have a hundredth part of the whole, and afterwards, for every hundred men, such a share as every private freebooter would have; that the commanding officer of every ship should have eight shares, beside what would be due to him on account of the money, provisions, & c. which he might have advanced for the fitting out of his vessels; that the chief surgeon should, in addition to his appointments, receive one hundred piasters out of the whole, for medicines; that the ship's carpenter, independently of his pay, should have a present of one hundred piasters. By the same agreement, the indemnities, already fixed in the general regulation for the loss of different limbs, were augmented; and particular rewards were established for every illustrious achievement, either in engagements or in the attacking of fortresses.

Until all these measures had been effectuated, Morgan did not announce his plan to his companions. He proposed nothing less than to attack Panama, that great and opulent city, where he hoped to find accumulated all those heaps of gold and silver which were annually sent, as a tribute, from America to Europe. The difficulties in executing such a plan were apparently innumerable. The chief obstacle was, the great distance of that city from the sea; and not an individual on board the fleet was acquainted with the road that led thither. To remedy this inconvenience, the admiral determined in the first instance to go to the island of St Catherine, where the Spaniards confined their criminals, and thence to provide themselves with guides.

The passage was rapid. Morgan landed in that island one thousand men; who, by threatening to put to death every one that refused to surrender so terrified the Spaniards that they speedily capitulated. It was stipulated that, to save at least the honour of the garrison, there should be a sham fight: in consequence of this, a very sharp fire ensued, from the forts on one side, and from the ships on the other; but on both sides the cannons discharged only powder. Farther, to give a serious appearance to this military comedy, the governor suffered himself to be taken, while attempting to pass from fort Jerome to another fort. Hence followed an apparent disorder. At the beginning, the crafty Morgan did not rely too implicitly on this feint; and to provide for every event, he secretly ordered his soldiers to load their fusees with bullets, but to discharge them in the air, unless they perceived some treachery on the part of the Spaniards. But his enemies adhered most faithfully to their capitulation: and this mock engagement, in which neither party was sparing of powder, was followed for some time with all the circumstances which could give it the semblance of reality. Ten forts surrendered, one after another, after sustaining a kind of siege or assault: and this series of successes did not cost the life of a single man, or even a scratch, on the part of the victors or of the conquered.

All the inhabitants of the island were shut up in the great fort of Santa Teresa, which was built on a steep rock: and the conquerors, who had not taken any sustenance for twenty-four hours, declared a most furious war against the horned cattle and game of the district.

In the Isle of St Constantine, he found four hundred and fifty-nine persons of both sexes; one hundred and ninety of whom were soldiers, forty-two criminals, eighty-five children, and six-six negroes. There were ten forts, containing sixty-eight cannons, and which were so defended in other respects by nature, that very small garrisons were deemed amply sufficient to protect them. Beside an immense quantity of fusees and grenades (which were at that time much used), upwards of three hundred quintals of gunpowder were found in the arsenal. The whole of this ammunition was carried on board the pirates' ships: the cannon, which could be of no service to them, were spiked; their carriages were burnt; and all the forts demolished excepting one, which the free-booters themselves garrisoned. Morgan selected three of the criminals to serve him as guides to Panama; and whom he afterwards, on his return to Jamaica, set at liberty; even giving them a share in the booty.

The plan, conceived by this intrepid chieftain, inspired all his companions in arms with genuine enthusiasm: it had a character of grandeur and audacity that enflamed their courage; how capable they were of executing it, the subsequent pages will demonstrate.

To be continued...

Resurrection Of A Highwayman

Patrick O'Brian, a native of Ireland, after committing a series of atrocities, was at length apprehended and executed at Gloucester for highway robbery; and when he had hung the usual time, his body was cut down, and given to his friends; but when carried home he was observed to move, on which a surgeon was immediately sent for, who bled him, and other means being used, he recovered life. This fact was kept a secret, and it was hoped that it would have a salutary effect upon his future conduct. His friends were very willing to contribute towards his support, in order that he might live in the most retired manner. He engaged to reform his life, and for some time kept his promise; but the impressions of death, and all the tremendous consequences, soon wearing off his mind, he returned to his vicious courses. Abandoning his friends, and purchasing a horse and other necessaries, he again visited the road.

In about a year after his execution, he met the same gentleman who was his former prosecutor, attacked him in the same manner as before. The gentleman was surprised to see himself stopped by the same person who had formerly robbed him, and who was executed for that crime. His consternation was so great, that he could not avoid acknowledging it, and asked him, 'How comes it to pass? I thought you had been hanged a twelvemonth ago.' 'So I was, and therefore you ought to imagine that what you now see is only my ghost. However, lest you shall be so uncivil as to hang my ghost too, I think it my best way to secure you.' Upon this he discharged a pistol through the gentleman's head, and alighting from his horse, cut his body in pieces with his hanger.

One barbarity was followed by a greater. O'Brian, accompanied by another four, attacked the house of Launcelot Wilmot, Esquire, of Wiltshire; entered and bound all the servants, then went up to the gentleman's own room, and bound him and his wife. They next proceeded to the daughter's chamber; used her in a brutal manner, and stabbed her to the heart. They then returned – in the same manner, butchered the old people, and rifled the houses to the value of two thousand five hundred pounds.

This miscreant continued his depredations two years longer, until one of his accomplices confessed his crime, and informed upon all who were concerned. Our adventurer was seized at his lodgings in Little Suffolk Street, and conveyed to Salisbury, where he acknowledged his crime. He was a second time executed, and, to prevent a second resurrection, he was hung in chains near the place where the crime was perpetrated.

Pressing To Death

The horrid punishment of pressing to death, which the English law imposes on persons standing mute when put on their trial, was frequently inflicted in former times, and some instances of it are even to be met with, of as late a date as the reign of George II.

At the Kilkenny assizes, in 1740, one Matthew Ryan was tried for highway robbery. When he was apprehended, he pretended to be a lunatic, stripped himself in the gaol, threw away his clothes, and could not be prevailed upon to put them on again, but went as he was to the court to take his trial. He then affected to be dumb, and would not plead; on which the judges ordered a jury to be impanelled, to inquire and give their opinion, whether he was mute and lunatic by the hand of God or wilfully so. The jury returned in a short time, and brought in a verdict of 'Wilful and affected dumbness and lunacy.' The judges on this desired the prisoner to plead; but he still pretended to be insensible to all that was said to him. The law now called for the peine forte et dure; but the judges compassionately deferred awarding it until a future day, in the hope that he might in the meantime acquire a juster sense of his situation. When again brought up however, the criminal persisted in his refusal to plead; and the court at last pronounced the dreadful sentence, that he should be pressed to death. This sentence was accordingly executed upon him two days after, in the public market of Kilkenny. As the weights were heaping on the wretched man, he earnestly supplicated to be hanged; but it being beyond the power of the sheriff to deviate from the mode of punishment prescribed in the sentence, even this was an indulgence which could no longer be granted to him.

In England, the latest instance (we believe) of a similar kind occurred in a case where Baron Thompson presided as judge. It is an odious and revolting mode of satisfying public justice; yet it is only a necessary adjunct to that fondness of capital punishments which pervades, and is a stain to the whole of the English penal code.

Confessions Of A Highwayman

Henry Simms was tried and executed for a highway robbery in 1745, after conviction he gave the following account of his exploits:

'I will begin,' says he, 'with my nativity. I was born in the parish of St Martin in the Fields, in the county of Middlesex, and should be thirty-one years of age, were I to live until next October; my parents who were honest people, died when I was an infant, and after their deaths, I was taken into the care of my grandmother, who lived in St James's parish, Westminster, who was the wife of a commissioned officer in his late majesty's land forces, and is still living, and receives a widow's pension from the crown.

This good old woman, when I was but six years of age, put me to school to one of her own religion, she being a Dissenter; but not approving of his way of teaching, she took me from him, and sent me to an academy in Charles-street, St James's, where I learnt arithmetic throughout, and some French and Latin; but frequently playing truant, I often ran into vice, before I was nine years of age, and frequently laid out nights, with other boys as wicked as myself; for which ill practices my grandmother used to correct me severely.

The first fact I ever committed was before I was ten years old. My Grandmother went to pay a visit to a Dissenting minister, at one Mr Palmer's, a soap-boiler, in Crown-court, St Anne's, and while she was in company with him, I got to the shop till, and took out about twenty shillings in silver, but was detected, and got a severe beating.

I frequently used to pick my grandmother's pocket of two or three shillings, which she seldom missed; or if she did suspect me, or challenge me with it, I had always something to say to prove me innocent. By my laying out of nights I soon got into bad company; and they led me to the worst of houses, particularly the Two-Penny Runs in St Giles's parish. This company persuaded me to rob my grandmother; and one morning, I opened a large chest in her house, and took away about £17 in gold and silver, and my best clothes, all which I carried to my new companions, and distributed the money very liberally amongst them, for which they greatly caressed me, made me drunk, and carried me to their house (as they called it) in Church-lane, St Giles's, where they put me to bed, and as soon as I was asleep, they stript me stark naked, leaving me alone; and when I awaked in the morning, I found they had left me nothing but rags to cover my nakedness.

What could I do, I could not tell, for it was impossible for me to go home to my grandmother's; at last I proposed to go to the Two-Penny Run in Vine-street, to enquire after my companions, but could hear nothing of them. The landlord took compassion on me, and gave me some victuals, and went to my grandmother's, to let her know where I was. The old gentlewoman came crying, ready to break her heart, and after being a little composed, she asked me what I had done with her money, and how I had disposed of my clothes? I told her several impudent lies, and seemed sorrowful for my fault, though I slily laughed in my sleeve to think I had bit the old woman. The landlord was more ingenuous than I was, and told her who had brought me thither. The names of my hopeful companions were Wry-neck Jack, George Monk, Nunkey Watson, and several more, all pilfering thieves, and petty pickpockets.

None of these gentry could be found; so the old gentlewoman took me with her, and caused me to be chained to the kitchen grate, with an iron chain and a padlock she had brought for that purpose; in which confinement I was continued for three months all day long, but was indulged with a bed in the night time, and a strict watch kept on me.

On my promise of amendment I got released, and more new clothes were bought me, which, when I got, I went to my old haunts, and this being the time of Tottenham-court fair, I went thither, and saw my companions tossing up for money. They soon recollected me, and were glad to see me, so I went with them to a music booth, where they made me almost drunk with gin, and began to talk their flash language, which I did not then understand.

Night coming on, and I wanting to go to sleep, they took me to a brick-kiln in Tottenham Court Road, and the kiln being burning, they broiled some meat, and made me eat part of it.

We had not been there long, before several women came to us, who were all very ragged; they brought with them a keg of gin, which they had stolen, and began to sing their flash songs, and I was as merry as the best of them.

The women were very fond of me, and being drunk, I began to swear, which pleased them wonderfully. One of them took a silk handkerchief out of her pocket, and taking off my stock, in which was a silver buckle, she put her handkerchief about my neck, and then unbuckled my shoes, and unbuttoned the knees of my breeches, and tied my garters below knee, telling me that was the way the Bowman boys wore them.

As soon as my companions found me asleep, they stript me of all my clothes, and everything else, except my shirt, and on their taking leave, threw some water over me, for when I awaked I found myself very wet, and almost perished with cold. I began to cry and lament sadly, when two or three women came up, and offered me their service to go and find out the people who had robbed me; and carried me to a place where they sift cinders, and got two old shoes, which I put on, and was going with them towards Tottenham-court Fair; but in the long field I saw my grandmother's man come running after me, upon some intelligence the old woman received where I was. On his seizing me the women ran away.

Being now at home with my grandmother, I behaved pretty well for some time; and she proposed to put me apprentice to a breeches-maker, one of her religion, and a very honest man. To him I was bound, but being lazy, wicked, and unruly, he beat me heartily, so I ran away from him in less than three weeks.

I went home to my grandmother, and taking an opportunity of her being abroad, I took all my best clothes, went to Rag-fair, and sold them, and spent the money among my old companions.

My grandmother finding I was not to be reclaimed, removed from her own house to lady St-nh-pe's, where she continued while her ladyship was in the country; and thither I went one night, and because I could not directly get admittance one night I broke a great many windows, and the old woman was at last obliged to let me in. There lived a silversmith next door, and one day, whilst the workmen were gone to dinner, I got over the wall, and stole a silver candlestick, and a stand for a tea-kettle, which I carried off, with all the lady's housekeeper's linen; and went directly to Mary-le-bone Park, to a barn, which my companions and I harboured in, where I found Jack Sutton, Jack Skinner, and two or three women, and to them I produced my booty; at the sight of which they seemed greatly rejoiced, and told me they were sure I should turn out a very promising young fellow. We sold the things in Peter-street, Soho, and had £9 for the plate and linen.

The plate being missed, my grandmother and several neighbours were after me, and I was seized in Paradise Row, Tyburn-road, and brought home, and threatened with justice; I confessed where the plate and the linen was sold, but the woman was gone, and could not be heard of, so they were never recovered. This affair was made up by means of lady St-nh-pe; but my grandmother for ever after excluded me that house; so I went to my old companions at Mary-le-bone, and concluded that night to rob any one we met; which we did, and picked up some small sums.

About a fortnight after I was taken up on suspicion of being concerned with them in divers robberies; and was committed to Newgate; but there being no proof against me, I was cleared at the sessions: my grandmother was so kind as to get me out of gaol and take me home, where I continued not long before I broke out again, and got acquainted with one Henry Chamberlain; who used to write incendiary letters; and he persuaded me to write a threatening letter to Mr Dawson in the Mint in the Tower, which I did, and demanded five guineas.

For this piece of villany, I was apprehended, and sent to the Tower gaol; but disguising my hand, and saying a man gave me a shilling to carry the letter, after three days confinement, and several examinations before the governor of the Tower, I was discharged.

My next acquaintance was with two brothers, named Toon, and one James Mahony, and we committed several robberies together: they were taken up and transported, but I had the good luck to escape; though their fate gave me some uneasiness; and I thought of relinquishing all vice, and told my grandmother my intention; and she promised if I would keep my word, she would love me more tenderly than ever; and on my faithful promise to do so, she took me home again; and I tarried with about four months; and did nothing but divert myself at duck-hunting and bear-baiting, where I got acquainted with thieves from all quarters of the town, who soon perverted me from my good resolutions.

Being one day washing in Mary-le-bone Basin, I perceived an elderly gentleman walking through the park, and up a bye-place, called the Bear-gardens, and following him, met with Jack Robinson, and Joe S------------e, and we agreed to rob him, and accordingly knocked him down, and took his silver watch, a gold ring, and about forty shillings in silver, tied him, and flung him into a ditch, left him, then made off, and divided the booty between us.

Abundance of my acquaintance being either transported or hanged, I began to think of another course of life, and being recommended to the late Mr Blunt, he hired me as a postillion. This business made me acquainted with almost all the roads in England; so that no one was ever better qualified for a highwayman than myself; and having a good share of impudence, I thought the highway would make me a gentleman at once; however, I deferred this dangerous undertaking for some time. After Mr Blunt's death, I served Mr Tatloe, who succeeded him; I was hired as a postillion to a noble duke, where I remained but a short time.

I now got again into very bad company about Covent-garden, and turned a great gamester, and was every night at my lord's, unless when I had no money, and then turned out to seek my fortune on the streets.

At the gaming table, I had good luck, and always appearing genteel, the gamblers gave me the name of Young Gentleman Harry. There was one Henry Moythen, whom they called Old Gentleman Harry, used the same table, and as he taught me to cheat at play, they insisted I should answer to his name. My father (as he was called) not long after our acquaintance, met with a very unlucky accident at a public house in Russell-street, Covent-garden, where having some words about a law suit with one Dick Hodges, a distiller, Hodges was so unkind as to run a knife into his guts, so that he was sent out of the world without having so much as having time to say his prayers.

I was very sorry to hear the news of my father's fatal catastrophe, but it was no more than I expected, for our acquaintance used to tell us, that neither of us would die in our beds; and now, to my sorrow, I find their words too true.

Amongst my many female acquaintances, on whom I spent my money and time, Will M-rg-----m's wife was my greatest favourite, though I got myself into some trouble on her account; for Will indicted me at the Old Bailey for a robbery; but the court finding there was a barrel better herring between the prosecutor and prisoner, I was acquitted and discharged from Newgate. To do justice to the woman, I shall take the whole blame on myself; I persuaded her to take the things, and they were as much her property as her pretended husband's.

Before this, I and Tom Casey had committed several robberies in the county of Kent, in 1743. The first robbery we did, was attacking a gentleman on Shooter's Hill, and robbing him of £17. About a week afterwards, I myself attacked a lady in her chariot upon Black heath, and took from her a purse with gold and silver in it, and two diamond rings. I was pursued by some butchers as far as Lewisham Water, who there dismounted me, tore off the cape of my coat, and were going to knock me down; but I recovering myself, presented my two pistols at them, on which they drew back, so that I made the best of my way along the road that leads to Newcross turnpike, leaving my horse, which was an exceedingly good gelding, behind me. I secreted myself in a corn field till after midnight, and then came to town. The purse and money I hid in a tree, and in a day or two fetched my store, and regaled plentifully till all was gone.

About this time the gaming table having very much reduced me, I got a horse, and went into the country, and at Towcester, in Northamptonshire, I put up at the White Horse. I spied an ancient gentleman in the kitchen, who had hired a chaise and two horses to bring him to London: a Welchman being to ride one of those horses, I thought this was a good chance, and asked the ostler who the man was. He said he had a commission in the army, but was a poor mean-spirited old rogue, for he had not given him a single farthing. Thought I, then there will be the more for me, for I was fully determined to turn him, and made myself ready to follow him as soon as he set forward from the inn. I was exceedingly well dressed, having on a green velvet coat, a gold laced hat and waistcoat, and every thing answerable; so that I could not be suspected for a highwayman. I observed that the old cuff had a brace of pistols in the chaise, and therefore determined to throw myself upon him, as soon as I could find an opportunity, and one soon presented itself; for the Welchman dismounting to fasten part of the harness which had given way, I rode up in a great hurry, and the old man called me, and said, 'Young man, if you ride so fast, you will soon ride your estate away.' I told him, 'I hoped not, for it was pretty extensive, and lay in several counties;' and immediately jumped from my horse and chaise, secured the pistols, and told the gentleman if he spoke one word, I would shoot him. I searched his pockets, and found seven shillings which I did not take; and in the seat of the chaise I found a pair of scarlet bags, which I mounted on my horse, and rode away furiously into the county of Bedfordshire.

At a proper place I examined the bags, and found some thread, stockings, three clean Holland shirts, two white waistcoats, and 102 guineas in gold. I was quite overjoyed, and after securing the money, threw the bags and the linen into a field, thinking they might be of some use to a poor countryman, who might have more need of them than me.

I was determined to reach London that night, and though my horse was greatly fatigued, yet he held out, and performed the journey very well. I went that night to my lord's, and began to flash my cole, and played high. Some who knew me said, 'Hal, who have you touched for the night;' I replied, 'I had been to receive a quarter's rent.' Three days after this robbery, as I was going out of town on pleasure, with some of my companions; just by Hyde Park turnpike, the Welchman, who drove the gentleman I had robbed, called out to me, and said, 'master, you never remembered your poor Welchman.' I instantly remembered the man's face, and beckoned him to me, and gave him a crown; so we parted, and he wished me a good journey. However, I did not much like him, and so persuaded my companions to turn back, without telling them the reasons I had for doing so.

This robbery being advertised in all the papers, and a particular description given of my person, I shipped myself on board a privateer, but soon ran away from the ship. I afterwards enlisted for a soldier, and now began to keep low company, having no money and but few clothes. I used to be constantly in brothels, and live on what I could get from poor creatures. At last, for almost beating a woman's eye out, I was sent to New Prison, from whence I broke out, but was soon taken, and carried to Covent-garden round house, and from hence before the late colonel De Veil, where I made an information for robbery against several persons, particularly, Robert Scott, Roger Allen, and William Bailey. The latter was taken up and tried for robbing Abraham Dirknell, servant to the duke of Bolton, of several goods, which were stolen from a stable belonging to his grace. I humbly ask pardon of God Almighty, and the poor injured men; for they were all innocent of this fact, and I committed the robbery and I really perjured myself on Bailey's trial, though he had the good fortune to be acquitted.

In my information before Sir Thomas De Veil, I accused William Cavenagh, Richard Smith, and William Gibbs, with breaking and entering the dwelling house of Mr Nathan Smith, of the borough of Southwark; but they all were innocent of that accusation, and it was at the instigation of the thief-takers that I swore against them. I was concerned in this robbery, but they were not; it was committed by me, Tom Casey, Will Bullimore, and Jack England, all Irishmen.

When the before-mentioned persons were acquitted at Croydon, of the robbery in Mr Smith's house, I was removed to Newgate, and tried at the Old Bailey, on my own information, for robbing a barber's shop; and being convicted was ordered for transportation, and soon after was put on board a ship in the river. On board the ship there was one Alexander Connell, an Irish boy; and he, with some others of the transports, promised to seize the captain and ship's company at Cowes in the Isle of Wight, but they watched us so strictly that we had no opportunity. The boatswain and I consulted to get away, but all to no purpose; so, after a tedious passage, we arrived at Anapolis in Maryland, where

I was sold for twelve guineas; but I gave my master the slip, and never lay one night in the country.

It happened luckily, that a horse on which my new master rode, was tied to a gate about a mile from the dwelling house, as an old negro informed me; and my master and the captain having been drinking pretty heavily, I took an opportunity of getting away in the night, whilst they were asleep; and by the assistance of this old negro, got the horse; and for the bribe of a guinea, which I had concealed, he directed me to the sea side, where I arrived, having rode thirty miles in less than four hours, through roads, some of which were almost impassable. When I saw the ocean about two miles distance, I dismounted, threw the horse's saddle and bridle away, and turned him loose in the woods. I then walked to the sea-side, and hailed the Two Sisters, James Abercrombie, master, who shipped me that night, and I was to have six guineas for the run home. In our passage we were taken by a privateer, called the Chacer, belonging to the Bayonne in France, and were carried into Oporto; I ran away from the ship, and secreted myself some days in the town, but was discovered, and pressed on board the King's Fisher, where I behaved so well, that in a short time I was made midshipman; but longing to come to my native country, I found means to get away from the ship, and walked to Lisbon, where I went onboard the Hanover Packet boat, and in less than twelve days arrived at Falmouth. Here I tarried upwards of a month with Jemmy Field, an old acquaintance, and spent what money I brought from Portugal in an idle manner.

When all I had was squandered away in a riotous manner, I shipped myself on board a coaster which traded to Bristol; the captain and I quarrelled, and I had like to have knocked him overboard. When we came to Bristol, he would not pay me my wages, but threatened to send me to Newgate in that city, on account of some money that I had borrowed from him; so I thought it the best way to escape in a whole skin, with about eight shillings in my pocket; and having hired a bridle and a saddle, I stole a horse out of a field, and rode away with him.

The first robbery I committed was near Cane, where I stopped a post-chaise and took from a gentleman and lady a silver watch, and £34 7s in money. The next robbery was near Hungerford, where I stopped the Bath coach, and took from a lady a diamond solitaire, three diamond rings, and some small trifle of money; and from the other passengers, about five guineas. I stopped a coach on the same road about three hours afterwards, and robbed an old gentleman of a silver tankard, tied in a handkerchief, and about forty shillings.

When I came to London, I saw the horse advertised which I had stole from Bristol, and putting up at the White Swan in Whitechapel, I was afraid to go for my horse, for fear I should be stopt. And going to St James, to see some of my acquaintance, I stole a horse from a boy in Rider-street, and rode away, but was stopped at Tyburn turnpike, and the toll-man knocked me off the horse, because he knew whose property it was; but on my presenting a pistol, I got away, but not without the loss of my hat and wig, and I was obliged to leave my horse behind me.

I went to Chelsea, and dined at the Cock. Next day I went to Mrs M------rg--n's, at Addlehill, and made her pawn her gown for eight shillings. I then went to Kingston upon Thames, and there hired a returned horse to Godalmin, but instead of going thither, I crossed Kingston Bridge; and on Smallberry green I saw a gentleman's servant who had hung his horse on a gate, while playing with a wench, so I exchanged horses. The next day I robbed the Worcester coach, near Gerrard's Cross, in Bucks, and from the passengers I took about twenty-five shillings.

The next robbery was of Mr Sleep, for which I am to die. That day I robbed seven farmers of about £18 and then came to London, and lay at the Greyhound in Drury Lane. Next day I went out and dined at Stratford, took a ride to Epping Forest, robbed Bess Watts of four diamond rings, and from a gentleman who rode in the chaise with her I took three guineas. On the forest I robbed Captain Bateman, the king's wheel-wright, of his gold watch, ten guineas, and about twenty-five shillings in silver. I did not shoot or rob the clergyman who was found dead in Epping Forest; I mention this, because many gentlemen have questioned me about it; I was at that time a close prisoner in Bedford gaol.

I intended to go over to Ireland, and setting out for St Albans, I got into company, and drank too much, and seeing the Warrington stage coach, I rode after it, and robbed the passengers; and, being drunk, I rode to Hockliffe in Bedfordshire, and put up at the Star inn, and sitting down in the kitchen, I fell fast asleep, and was taken by some troopers, on a hue and cry, for robbing the coach. I was confined close in the house that night, and all my money taken from me, but I had got Bess Watt's rings, tied up in a knot of my neck-cloth, and the troopers not finding them, I that night swallowed them in the skin of a duck's leg, which I well rubbed with butter. These rings I afterwards gave Irish Peg to dispose of when I was confined in Bedford gaol; but she was taken up, and tried at Gloucester, and punished there; and Bess Watts had her rings again.

The night I was seized I attempted to kill one of the troopers who guarded me, and he was endeavouring to take the seal of Captain Bateman's watch out of the fire, which I had purposefully thrown to make him stoop; but my pistol missing fire, the man saved his life. They then tied my hands, and carried me before justice Nodes of Luton in Bedfordshire, who committed me; and in Bedford gaol I was collared with an iron collar, and had shears on my legs, so I could hardly stir; though if the habeas corpus had not come to remove me to Newgate, I should have slipt through their fingers, for a female acquaintance could have released me in a day or two.

Being brought to Newgate, I was tried at the Old Bailey, and justly convicted for robbing Mr Sleep. All those I have offended I hope will forgive me, and God Almighty receive my soul.'

The information he made relating to his being hired to shoot his majesty, had not the least foundation, and his only view in it was to prolong his life.

Simms, whilst under sentence, behaved very undauntedly, especially before he was certain of death. He quarrelled with Mary Allen, another convict, and beat her very much: but when the warrant came down, he was more orderly, and seemed greatly shocked.

Adventures Of Morgan, Prince of Free-Booters: The Treasures of Panama

Continued from page 83…

Panama, which stood on the shore of the South Sea, in the 9th degree of northern latitude, was at that time one of the greatest, as well as the most opulent cities in America. It contained two thousand large houses, the greater number of which were very fine piles of building, and five thousand smaller dwellings, each mostly three stories in height. Of these, a pretty considerable number were erected of stone, all the rest of cedar wood, very elegantly constructed and magnificently furnished. The city was defended by a rampart, and was surrounded with walls. It was the emporium for the silver of Mexico, and the gold of Peru; whence those valuable metals were brought on the backs of mules (two thousand of which animals were kept for this purpose only), across the isthmus towards the northern coast of the South Sea. A great commerce was also carried on at Panama in negroes; which trade was at the time almost exclusively confined to the English, Dutch, French, and Danes. With this branch of commerce the Italians were intimately connected, who gave lessons in it to all the rest of Europe; and, as two things were necessary (in which the Genoese were by no means deficient), – money and address,– they were chiefly concerned in the slave trade, and supplied the provinces of Chili and Peru with negroes.

At the period now referred to, the president of Panama was the principal intendant or overseer of the civil department, and the captain-general of all troops in the vice-royalty of Peru. He had in his dependency Porto Bello and Nata, two cities inhabited by the Spaniards, together with the towns of Cruces, Panama, Capira, and Veragua. The city of Panama had also a bishop, who was a suffragan of the archbishop of Lima.

The merchants lived in great opulence; and their churches were decorated with uncommon magnificence. The cathedral was erected in the Italian style, surmounted with a large cupola, and enriched with gold and silver ornaments; as also were the eight convents, which this city comprised. At a small distance from its walls, there were some islands alike embellished by art and by nature, where the richest inhabitants had their country houses; from which circumstance they were called the gardens of Panama. In short, everything concurred to render this place important and agreeable. Here several of the European nations had palaces for carrying on their commerce; and among these were the Genoese, who were held in great credit, and who had vast warehouses for receiving the articles of their immense trade, as also a most magnificent edifice. The principal houses were filled with beautiful paintings, and the master-pieces of the arts, which had here been accumulated, more from an intense desire of being surrounded with all the splendour of luxury (since they possessed the means of procuring it), than from a refined taste. Their superabundance of gold and silver had been employed in obtaining these splendid superfluities; which were of no value, but to gratify the vanity of their possessors.

Such was Panama in 1670, when the free-booters selected it as the object of their bold attempt, and as the victim of their extravagancies; and immortalized their name by reducing it to a heap of ruins.

In the execution of this design, which stupefied the New World, they displayed equal prudence and cruelty. Previous to the adoption of any other measure, it was necessary that the Pirates should get possession of fort St Laurent, which was situated on the banks of the river Chagre. With this view Morgan dispatched four ships, with four hundred men, under the command of the intrepid Brodely, who had succeeded in victualling the fleet, and who was intimately acquainted with the country. Morgan continued at the island of St Catherine with the rest of his forces. His plan was to dissemble his vast projects against Panama, as long as it was possible, and to cause the pillage of the fort St Laurent to be regarded as a common expedition to which he would confine himself.

Brodely discharged this commission with equal courage and success. That castle was situated in a lofty mountain, at the mouth of a river, and was inaccessible on almost every side. The first attempts were fruitless; and the free-booters, who advanced openly, without any other arms than fusees and sabres, at first lost many of their comrades: for the Spaniards not only made use of all their artillery and musketry against them, but were also seconded by the Indians that were with them in the fort, and whose arrows were far more fatal than bullets. The assailants saw their companions in arms fall by their side, without being able to avenge them. The danger of their present situation, and the nature of their arms, seemed to render the enterprise altogether impracticable. Their courage began to waver; their ranks were thrown into disorder, and they already thought of retiring, when the provocations of the Spaniards inspired them with new vigour. 'You heretic dogs,' cried they in a triumphant tone: 'You cursed English, possessed by the devil! Ah! you will go to Panama! will you? No, no; that you shall not; you shall all bite the dust here; and all your comrades shall share the same fate.'

From these insulting speeches the pirates learnt that the design of their expedition was discovered; and that moment they determined to carry the fort, or die to a man on the spot. They immediately commenced the assault in defiance of the shower of arrows that was discharged against them; undismayed by the loss of their commander, both whose legs had been carried away by a cannon shot. One of the pirates, in whose shoulder an arrow was deeply fixed, tore it out himself, exclaiming:– 'Patience, comrades, and it strikes me, all the Spaniards are lost!' He tore some cotton out of his pocket, with which he covered his ram-rod, set the cotton on fire, and shot this burning material, in lieu of bullets, at the houses of the fort, which was covered with light wood, and the leaves of palm trees. His companions collected together the arrows which were strewed around them on the ground, and employed them in a similar manner. The effect of this novel mode of attack was most rapid: many of the houses caught fire; a powder wagon blew up. The besieged, being thus diverted from their means of defence, thought only of stopping the progress of the fire. Night came on: under cover of darkness, the freebooters attempted also to set on fire the palisades, which were made of a kind of wood that was easily kindled. In this attempt likewise they were crowned with success; the soil, which the palisades supported, fell down, and filled up the ditch. The Spaniards nevertheless continued to defend themselves with much courage, being animated by the example of their commander, who fought till the very moment he received a mortal blow. The garrison had throughout the use of their cannon, which kept up a most violent fire; but the enemy had already made too much progress to be disconcerted with it; they persevered in the attack, until they at length became masters of the fort.

A great number of Spaniards, finding themselves deprived of all resource, precipitated themselves from the top of the walls in to the river, that they might not fall alive into the hands of these freebooters; who made only twenty-four prisoners, and ten of these were wounded men, who had concealed themselves among the dead, in the hope of escaping their ferocious conquerors. These twenty-four men were all that remained of three hundred and forty, who had composed the garrison, which had shortly before been reinforced; for the president of Panama, having been apprized from Carthagena of the object of the pirates' expedition, came to encamp, with three thousand six hundred men in the vicinity of that threatened city. This information was conveyed to the freebooters, after the capture of the fort. At the same time they learnt that, among this body of troops, there were four hundred horsemen, six hundred Indians, and two hundred mulattoes; the last of whom, being very expert in hunting bulls, were intended, in case of necessity, to send two thousand of these animals among the freebooters.

It is scarcely credible that Brodely continued to command, notwithstanding the severity of his wounds; but he would not, by retiring, compromise the advantages he had so dearly purchased; for out of four hundred men who had composed his little army, one hundred and eighty had been killed, and eighty wounded, and of these eighty, sixty were altogether out of the battle.

The bodies of the French and English were interred; but those of the Spaniards were thrown down from the top of the fort, and remained in a heap at the foot of the walls. Brodely found much ammunition, and abundance of provisions; with which he was the more satisfied, as he knew that the grand fleet was greatly in want of both those articles. He caused the fort to be rebuilt, as far as it was practicable, in order that he might defend himself there, in case the Spaniards should make a speedy attempt to retake it. In this situation he waited for Morgan, who in a short time appeared with his fleet.

As the pirates approached, they beheld the English flag flying on the fort, and abandoned themselves to the most tumultuous joy and excessive drinking, without dreaming of the dangers occurring at the mouth of the river Chagre, beneath whose waters there was sunken rock. The coasting pilots of those latitudes came to their assistance; but their intoxication and impatience would not permit them to attend to the latter. This negligence was attended with the most fatal consequences, and cost them four ships, one of which was the admiral's vessel. The crews, however, together with their ladings, were saved. This loss greatly affected Morgan, who was wholly intent upon his vast designs; but who, nevertheless, made his entrance into St Laurence, where he left a garrison of five hundred men. He also detached from his body of troops one hundred and fifty men, for the purpose of seizing several Spanish vessels that were in the river.

The remainder of the forces Morgan directed to follow him... At length, on the eighteenth day of January, he commenced his march towards Panama, with a chosen body of freebooters, who were thirteen hundred strong. *To be continued...*

The Japanese Widow

A woman was left a widow with three sons, and with no other subsistence than their labour. The young men not having been brought up to this kind of life, could scarcely earn the most common necessities of life, and bitterly lamented their inability to place their mother in a more comfortable situation.

It had lately been decreed that any person who should seize a robber, and convey him to a magistrate, should receive a considerable reward. The three brothers, who were a thousand times more affected by their mother's poverty than their own, took a resolution as strange as heroic. They agreed that one of the three should pass as a robber, and the other two should denounce him as such: they drew lots to determine which was to be the victim of filial love, and it fell to the youngest, who was bound, and conducted to the magistrate as a criminal. He was questioned, confessed the robbery of which he was accused, was sent to prison, and the brothers received the reward; but before they returned home, they found means to enter the prison, wishing at least to bid an affectionate adieu to their unfortunate brother. There, believing themselves unobserved, they threw themselves into the arms of the prisoner, and by their tears, their sobs, and their most tender embraces, displayed the excess of their affection and grief. The magistrate, who by chance was in a place from whence he could perceive them, was extremely surprised to see a criminal receive such marks of affection from the very men who had delivered him up to justice, and he gave orders to follow the two young men, and observe them narrowly.

The servant reported to his master that he had followed the two young men to the door of their mother's apartment; that on entering, their first care was to give their mother the sum of money which they had received; that she, astonished at the sight of so considerable a sum, had shown more uneasiness than pleasure at it, and eagerly questioned them as to how they obtained it, and the cause of their brother's absence; that for a time the two youths could answer only with tears, but that at last, threatened by the malediction of a mother so tenderly beloved, they had confessed the truth. At this dreadful recital, the unfortunate woman, penetrated with gratitude, terror and admiration, and abandoning herself to the most violent transports of despair, sprang towards the door to go out, with the intention of declaring every thing to the magistrate; but that restrained by her cruelly generous sons, overwhelming them with reproaches, and bathing them with tears, overpowered at once by anger, and by the most passionate grief and tenderness, she had fallen senseless in their arms.

After this recital, the judge repaired to the prison, and questioned the younger brother, who still persisted in his account, and nothing could induce him to retract. The magistrate at last told him, that he wished to know to what extent of heroism filial piety could raise a virtuous heart, and declared to him he was informed of the truth. The judge went to report this adventure to the sovereign, who struck with an action so heroic, desired to see the three brothers and the happy mother of such virtuous children: he loaded them with praises and marks of distinction, assigned to the youngest 1,500 crowns a year, and 500 each to the other two.

The Cave of Clatto

The Lands of Clatto are most remarkable on account of the robberies said to have been committed on them when possessed by a family called Seaton. What is called Clatto Den is a den with steep banks. In the face of one of these is said to have been a cave, the mouth of which is now covered by the falling in of the soil, but it communicated with the old Castle or Tower of Clatto, the remains of which are visible at no great distance. The cave is said to have had another opening towards the road; and there the heedless traveller, being suddenly seized, was dragged into the cavern, from which nobody returned.

The ruin of the family of robbers that possessed the castle and the cave is ascribed by tradition to the following event. King James the Fourth accidentally passed that way alone, and was attacked by a son of Seaton, who stopped his horse. The king, though apparently unarmed, had a sword concealed under his garment, which he drew, and with a blow cut off the right hand that had seized his horse's reins. The robber instantly fled into a cavern, and the king, taking up the hand, rode off. Next day, attended by a strong retinue, he visited the Castle of Clatto, under pretence of seeing Seaton and his sons, who had been represented as enterprising men, well calculated to hold public employments. The old man presented his family to the king, but one of his sons was absent, and he was said to be unwell, in consequence of a hurt he had accidentally received. The king insisted on seeing him, and desired to feel his pulse. The young man held out his left hand; the king would feel the other also. After many ineffectual excuses, he was obliged to confess that he had lost his right hand. The king told him that he had a hand in his pocket, which was at his service, if it would fit him. Upon this, according to the barbarous mode of administering justice in those times, they were all seized and executed.

107

Adventures of Morgan, Prince of Free-booters: Attacked By Wild Bulls!

Continued from page 104…

On January 27th, 1671, which was the tenth of their march, the pirates advanced at a very early hour, with their military music, and took the road leading to Panama. By the advice, however, of one of the guides, they quitted the main road, and went out of the way across a thick wood, through which there was no foot-path. For this the Spaniards were unprepared; having confined themselves to the erection of batteries, and the construction of redoubts, on the highway. They soon perceived the inutility of this measure, and were obliged to relinquish their guns, in order to oppose their enemies on the contrary side; but, not being able to take their cannons away from their batteries, they were consequently incapacitated from making use of one part of their defensive means.

After two hours' march, the freebooters discovered the hostile army, which was a very fine one, well equipped, and was advancing in battle array. The soldiers were clad in party-coloured silk stuffs, and the horsemen were strutting on their mettlesome steeds, as if they were going to a bull fight. The president in person took command of this body of troops, which was of considerable importance, both for the country, and likewise for the forces supported there by Spain. He marched against the pirates with four regiments of the line, consisting of infantry, besides two thousand four hundred foot soldiers of another description, four hundred horsemen, and two thousand four hundred wild bulls under the conduct of several hundred Indians and negroes.

The army, which extended over the whole plain, was discovered by the pirates from the summit of a small eminence, and presented to them a most imposing appearance, insomuch that they were struck with a kind of terror. They began now to feel some anxiety as to the event of an engagement with forces so greatly superior in point of numbers; but they were convinced that they must either conquer or die, and encouraged each other to fight until the very last drop of their blood was shed; a determination this, which, on the part of these intrepid men, was by no means a vain resolution.

They divided themselves into three bodies, placed two hundred of their best marksmen in the front, and marched boldly against the Spaniards, who were drawn up in order of battle in a spacious plain. The governor immediately ordered the cavalry to charge the enemy, and the wild bulls to be at the same time let loose upon them. But the ground was unfavourable for the purpose; the horsemen encountered nothing but marshes, behind which were posted two hundred marksmen, who kept up a continual and well directed fire, that horses and men fell in heaps beneath their shots, before it was possible to effect a retreat. Fifty horsemen only escaped this formidable discharge of musketry. The bulls, on whose services they had calculated so highly, it became impracticable to drive against the pirates. Hence such a confusion arose as completely reversed the whole plan of the battle. The freebooters in consequence attacked the Spanish infantry with so much the greater vigour; they successively knelt on the ground, fired, and rose up again. While those, who were on one knee, directed their fire against the hostile army, which began to waver, the pirates, who continued standing, rapidly charged their fire-arms. Every man, on this occasion, evinced a dexterity and presence of mind which decided the fate of the battle; almost every shot was fatal.

The Spaniards nonetheless continued to defend themselves with much valour, which provided of little service against an exasperated enemy; whose courage, inflamed by despair, derived additional strength from their successes. At length the Spaniards had recourse to their last expedient; the wild bulls were let loose upon the rear of the freebooters. The former never dreamt that these had, in this expedition, associated with the Buccaneers, who had for a long time been accustomed to act against these animals: and this attack, which was to be decisive, frustrated all their plans. The Buccaneers were in their element; by their shouts they intimidated the bulls, at the same time waving party-coloured flags before them, fired on the animals, and laid them upon the ground without exception. The engagement lasted two hours; and notwithstanding the Spaniards were so greatly superior in both numbers and arms, it terminated entirely in favour of the freebooters. The Spaniards lost the chief part of their cavalry, on which they built their expectations of victory; the remainder returned to the charge repeatedly, but their efforts only tended to render their defeat the more complete. A very few horsemen only escaped, together with the ruins of the infantry, who threw down their arms to facilitate the rapidity of their flight. Six hundred Spaniards lay dead on the field of battle; besides whom, they sustained a considerable loss in such as were wounded and taken prisoners.

Among the latter were some Franciscans, who had exposed themselves to the greatest dangers, in order that they might animate the combatants, and afford the last consolations of religion to the dying. They were conducted into Morgan's presence, who instantly pronounced sentence of death upon them. In vain did these hapless religeuse implore that pity, which they might have claimed from a less ferocious enemy! They were all killed by pistol shot. Some Spaniards who were apprehensive lest they should be overtaken in their flight, had concealed themselves among the flags and rushes along the banks of the river. They were mostly discovered, and hacked to pieces by the merciless pirates.

The freebooters task, however, was by no means executed; they had yet to take Panama, a large and populous city, which was defended by forts and batteries, and into which the governor had retired, together with the fugitives. The conquest of this place was the more difficult, as the pirates had dearly purchased their victory, and the remaining forces were by no means adequate to encounter the difficulties attending such an enterprise. It was, however, determined to make an attempt. Morgan had just procured, from a wounded captive Spanish officer, the necessary information; but he had not a moment to lose. It would not do to allow the Spaniards time to adopt new measures of defence; the city was therefore assaulted on the same day, in defiance of a formidable artillery, which committed great havoc among the freebooters; and, at the end of three hours, they were in possession of Panama.

The capture of that city was followed by a general pillage. Morgan, who dreaded the consequences of excessive intoxication, especially after his men had suffered such a long abstinence, prohibited them from drinking wine, under the severest penalties. He foresaw that such a prohibition would infallibly be infringed, unless it was sanctioned by an argument far more powerful then the fear of punishment; he therefore caused it to be announced, that he had received information that the Spaniards had poisoned all their wine. This dexterous falsehood had the desired effect: and, for the first time, the freebooters were temperate.

The majority of the inhabitants of Panama had betaken themselves to flight; they had embarked their women, their riches, and their moveables that were of any value, and small in bulk, and had sent this valuable cargo to the island of Taroga. The men were dispersed over the continent, but in sufficiently large numbers to appear formidable to the pirates; whose forces were much diminished, and who could not expect any assistance from abroad. They therefore continued constantly together; and, for their greater security, most of them encamped without the walls.

We have now reached a time when Morgan committed a barbarous and incomprehensible action; concerning which his comrades (some of whom were his historians), have given only a very ambiguous explanation.

Notwithstanding all the precious articles had been carried away from Panama, there still remained, as in every great European trading city, a vast number of shops, warehouses, and magazines, filled with every kind of merchandise. Besides a great quantity of wrought and manufactured articles, the productions of luxury and industry, that city contained immense stores of flour, wine, and spices; vast magazines of that metal which is justly deemed the most valuable of all, because it is the most useful, extensive buildings, in which were accumulated prodigious stores of iron tools and implements, anvils, and ploughs, which had been received from Europe, and were destined to revive the Spanish colonies. Some judgement may be formed, respecting the value of the last-mentioned articles only, when it is considered that a quintal (1 cwt.) of iron was sold at Panama for thirty-two piasters (about £6 12s).

All these multifarious articles, so essentially necessary for the furnishing of an hemisphere with provisions, were (it would seem) of no value in the estimation of the ferocious Morgan, because he could not carry them away; although, by preserving them, he might have made use of them to demand a specific ransom for them. Circumstances might also enable him to derive some further advantages from them; but, in fact, whatever was distant, or uncertain, presented no attraction to this barbarian, who was eager to enjoy, but most ardent to destroy. He was struck with one consideration only. All these bulky productions of art and industry were, for the moment, of no use to the freebooters. Of what importance to him was the ruin of many thousand innocent families? He consulted only the ferocity of his character; and, without communicating his design to any individual, he secretly caused the city to be set on fire in several places. In a few hours it was almost entirely consumed. The Spaniards that had continued to Panama, as well as the pirates themselves, who were at first ignorant from whence the conflagration proceeded, ran together, and united their efforts in order to extinguish the flames. They brought water, and pulled down houses, with a view to prevent the further progress of that destructive element.

All their exertions were fruitless. A violent wind was blowing; and, in addition to this circumstance, (as already intimated), the principal part of the buildings in that city were constructed with wood. Its finest houses, together with their valuable furniture, among which was the magnificent palace belonging to the Genoese, the churches, convents, court-houses, shops, hospitals, pious foundations, warehouses filled with merchandize,— all were reduced to ashes! The fire also consumed a great number of beasts, horses, mules, and many slaves, who had concealed themselves, and who were burnt alive. A very few houses only escaped the fire, which continued burning upwards of four weeks. Amidst the havoc produced in every quarter by the conflagration, the free-booters did not neglect to pillage as much as they possibly could; by which means they collected a considerable booty.

Morgan seemed ashamed of his atrocious resolution; he carefully concealed that he had ever adopted it, and gave out that the Spaniards themselves had set their city on fire. In the morning it was nothing but a heap of ashes. A retired quarter, however, which was poor, wretchedly built, and occupied only by muleteers, was spared by the flames; as also were two convents, and the palace belonging to the president, which was sheltered by its remote situation.

After this deplorable catastrophe, the pirates assembled together, and entrenched themselves under the ruins of a church. Morgan detached a large body of well armed troops to go and announce his victory to those who had been left behind at Chagre, and to inform them of their situation. He likewise sent out two other detachments, of one hundred men each, to collect and bring in prisoners: he further sent out a well manned ship to cruise in the South Sea, and attempt the capture of some prizes there. This vessel, in fact, returned at the end of three days, with three ships that had been taken; but brought, at the same time, some information which extremely chagrined both the pirates and their chieftain. A large galleon had escaped their vigilance, which was laden with the treasures of the churches, as well as with a large quantity of silver, gold, and other precious articles, belonging to the king and the most opulent traders of Panama. On board this galleon also were the wives of the principal inhabitants, together with all their jewels, and every other article that could possibly be conveyed away. They had also succeeded in embarking on board a great number of children, and all the religeuse in the city. She had no other cargo, and did not even carry any ballast; or rather, the ingots of gold and silver supplied the place of ballast. This vessel, although laden with so many objects, the preservation of which was of such vast moment, was defended by no more than six guns and a scanty crew; besides which, she was in other respects but indifferently provided. She was sailing very securely: for, as the free-booters had arrived by land, the Spaniards were fully persuaded they could undertake nothing by sea.

It seemed impossible for a prize of such immense consequence to escape the rapacity of those corsairs. They discovered her, towards evening, at some distance from them; and had the address to intercept, without being discovered, the ship's boat, on board which were seven persons, from whom they received information highly necessary for the furtherance of their designs. From this moment, Chart, who was the commander of the pirate ship, considered the capture of the galleon as infallible; he waited only for the return of day, that he might take possession of her. It would otherwise have been impossible to attempt a capture, easy as it might appear, during the night. His crew, who were abundantly stocked with wine, and who had been in quest of women and girls in the small islands that lay in the vicinity of Panama, were so given up to excess of intoxication and debauchery, that, for the moment, they were incapacitated from firing at her. On the following day they had cause to repent of this forced delay, the consequences of which were irreparable. He still entertained hopes of overtaking the galleon; but she was now completely out of his reach. What despair must his comrades have experienced, on seeing that their negligence had deprived them of such a valuable prey; and that a few inconsiderable prizes constituted the whole fruit of their cruise!

To be continued…

Desolate Island

Alexander Selkirk, who was four years and four months by himself, on the island of Jaun Fernandez, said he was a native of Largo, in the county of Fife, in Scotland, and was bred a sailor from his youth; and, at the time he was left on the island, was master of a trading vessel called The Cinque Port, Captain Stradling commander.– The reason of his being left on the island, was a difference between him and Captain Stradling, and the ship being leaky, made him at first willing to stay there rather than go with him, but afterwards he changed his mind, and would gladly have gone on board again, but the Captain would not receive him. He had with him his clothes and bedding; also a firelock, a pound of powder, some bullets and some tobacco; a hatchet, a kettle, a knife; a bible, some books on practical divinity, and his mathematical instruments and books.

For the first eight months he was extremely melancholy, and could hardly support the terror of being alone in a desolate place.

He built himself two huts of pimento trees, covered with long grass, and lined with the skins of goats which he killed with his gun as long as his powder lasted. He got fire by rubbing two sticks of pimento wood together on his knee. In the smallest hut, which was some distance from the other, he dressed his victuals, and in the other he slept, and employed himself in reading, singing psalms, and praying; so that he said he was a better Christian whilst in this solitude, than he was before. When he was first left in this place he ate nothing until mere hunger obliged him, partly from the want of bread and salt, and partly from excess of grief; nor did he go to bed till the want of sleep would not permit him to stay longer awake.

The pimento wood, which burnt very clear, served him both for fire and candle, and refreshed him with its fragrant smell. He could have procured fish enough, but he could not eat them for want of salt, except a sort of cray fish, which was extremely good, and as large as our lobsters, – these he sometimes broiled, and at other times boiled; as he also did the goat's flesh, and made very good broth of it; for the taste of it is much more pleasant than that of the goats of England or Wales.– He kept an account of five hundred of these animals, which he had killed, and as many more which he caught and having marked them on the ear let them go again. When his powder was gone, he took them by out running them; for his way of living, and his continual exercise, walking and running, had so cleared his body of gross humours that he ran, with wonderful swiftness, through the woods, and up the rocks and hills. He distanced and tired both the swiftest runners belonging to the ship, and a bull-dog they had, in catching the goats, and bringing them on his back.

He once pursued a goat with so much eagerness that he caught hold of it on the brink of a precipice, of which he was not aware, as the bushes concealed it from his sight; so that he fell with the goat down the precipice, a prodigious height. He was so much hurt by the fall that he lay insensible, as he imagined, about twenty-four hours; and when he came to himself, he found the goat dead under him. He was hardly able to crawl to his hut, about a mile distant; nor was he able to go abroad again for two days.

He used to divert himself with cutting his name on the trees, together with the time of his being left and continuance there. He was at first much pestered with rats, which had bred, in great numbers, from some which had got on shore from ships which had put in there for food or water. The rats gnawed his feet and clothes while he slept, so that he was obliged to cherish some cats, which had also bred from some that had got on shore from ships that had put in there; these he fed on goats flesh, by which many of them became so tame, that they would lie about him in hundreds, and soon delivered him from the rats. He likewise tamed some kids, and to divert himself, he would frequently sing and dance with them and his cats; so that by the favour of Providence, and the vigour of his youth, he being now only thirty years of age, he was at length able to conquer all the inconveniences of his solitude, and became extremely easy.

When his clothes had worn out, he made himself a coat and a cap of goat's skin, which he sewed with little thongs of the same, cut with his knife. He had no other needle but a nail; and when his knife was worn out, he made others as well as he could of some iron hoops that were left ashore. Having some linen by him, he cut out some shirts, which he sewed with the worsted of some old stockings; he had his last shirt on when he was found. At his first going aboard, he seemed much rejoiced; but had so far forgot his native language for want of use, that he could not speak plainly, only dropping a few words now and then, without much connection; but in two or three days he began to talk, and then told them that his silence was involuntary, for being so long without any person to converse with, he had forgot the use of his tongue. A dram was offered him, but he refused to taste it, having drunk nothing but water for so long a time; and it was some time before he could relish the victuals on board.

A Hardened Convict

Two men were once convicted of highway robbery before Judge Caulfield. When the jury brought in their verdict of guilty, the elder of the two felons turned round to the younger, and, with a countenance expressive of the most diabolical rage, malice, and revenge, addressed his companion in the following manner:- 'Perdition seize you, you hen-hearted villain; if it had not been for you, I would have sent the rascal to hell who bore witness against us. I would have murdered the villain, and then he could have told no tales. But you, you cowardly scoundrel! persuaded me to let him go. You dog, if I am hanged, you will be hanged with me, and that is the only comfort and satisfaction I have. But, good people, if any of my profession be among you, take warning by my example. If you rob a man, kill him on the spot; you will then be safe, for dead men tell no tales. I have robbed many persons, and I may escape from prison and rob many more; and, by Heaven! the man I rob, I will surely murder.'

'May God visit the blood of the man you murder upon my head,' said Judge Caulfield. 'Go, Mr Sheriff, procure a carpenter, have a gallows erected, and a coffin made, on the very spot where the monster stands; for from the bench I will not remove, until I see him executed. As for the young man, whose heart, though corrupted by the influence of this infernal wretch, still retained the principles of humanity, he shall not perish with him. I must, indeed, pass upon him the sentence the law requires; but I will respite him, and use my influence with the crown to pardon.—This hoary villain shall not have the satisfaction which his malignant heart had anticipated.' The Sheriff obeyed the order – a gallows was erected in the court-house, and in the presence of the judge, the jury, and the people, the monster ascended the scaffold, cursing and blaspheming to the moment when he was launched into eternity.

Horrible Cruelty of Graeme, The Outlaw of Galloway

From the history of Galloway we extract the following account of the barbarous revenge of a ruffian, named Graeme, who was a celebrated freebooter of that country, and of whom many acts of bloody cruelty, too gross to be mentioned, are on record.

In an excursion this outlaw once made to plunder the lands of Gordon of Muirfad, he met with a notable defeat; for the old laird, aware of his intentions, had collected a body of his friends and dependants together; and these being placed in ambush, Graeme was taken completely by surprise, a number of his gang killed, and himself seriously wounded. Stung with rage and shame at being thus foiled, where he did not expect even resistance, he vowed a deadly vengeance: nor was it long protracted; for, watching his opportunity, he appeared so suddenly before the castle, with a strong force, that those within were taken quite unprepared. What they could do they did: they secured the gates, or rather doors, for it never could have been a place capable of making much resistance. Graeme demanded

admission, uttering the most dreadful threats in case of a refusal. Gordon, sensible of his own weakness, was desirous of entering into some compromise with the robbers, and, for that purpose, solicited a parley at the door, against which Graeme had, by this time, piled up faggots and brush-wood for the purpose of setting it on fire. A sum of money in the meantime, and a future annuity, by way of black-meal, for protection, or rather forbearance, were the terms agreed on.

The arrangements having been finally made, Graeme observed that they might as well part friends: and advancing to the grated window, in the centre of the door through which they had carried out their negotiations, and having received the stipulated sum, he held out his hand at parting. As this was a piece of courtesy which could not be declined with safety, the proffered symbol of amity was accepted. No sooner, however, were their hands joined, than Graeme, throwing a noose over the other's wrist, pulled with all his might, till an iron staple was driven into the wall, to which he fastened the end of the chain, and instantly setting fire to the pile, burnt him alive behind his door;– the castle and all it contained being destroyed.

Terrific Love

Avilda, daughter of the King of Gothland, contrary to the manner and disposition of her sex, exercised the profession of piracy, and was scouring the seas with a powerful fleet, while a sovereign was offering sacrifices to her beauty at the shrine of love. King Sigar perceiving that this masculine lady was not to be gained by the usual arts of lovers, took the extraordinary resolution of addressing himself in a mode more agreeable to her humour. He fitted out a fleet, went in quest of her, engaged her in a furious battle, which continued two days without intermission, and thus gained possession of a heart to be conquered only by valour.

The Villainous Innkeeper

In 1742, a gentleman in travelling was stopped by a highwayman in a mask, within about seven miles of Hull, and robbed of a purse containing twenty guineas. The gentleman proceeded about two miles further, and stopped at the Bull Inn, kept by Mr Brunell. He related the circumstances of the robbery, adding, that as all his gold was marked, he thought it probable that the robber would be detected. After he had supped, his host entered the room, and told him a circumstance had arisen which led him to think he could point out the robber. He then informed the gentleman that he had a waiter, one John Jennings, whose conduct had long been very suspicious; he had long before dark sent him out to change a guinea for him, and said that he had only come back since he (the gentleman) was in the house, saying he could not get change; that Jennings being in liquor, he sent him to bed, resolving to discharge him in the morning; that at the same time he returned with the guinea, he discovered it was not the same he had given him, but was marked, of which he took no further notice until he heard the particulars of the robbery, and that the guineas which the highwayman had taken were all marked. He added, that he had unluckily paid away the marked guinea to a man who lived at some distance.

Mr Brunell was thanked for his information, and it was resolved to go softly to the room of Jennings, whom they found fast asleep; his pockets were searched, and from one of them was drawn a purse containing exactly nineteen guineas, which the gentleman identified. Jennings was dragged out of bed and charged with the robbery. He denied it most solemnly; but the facts having been deposed on oath by the gentleman and Mr Brunell, he was committed for trial.

So strong did the circumstances appear against Jennings, that several of his friends advised him to plead guilty, and throw himself on the mercy of the court. This advice he rejected; he was tried at the ensuing assizes, and the jury, without going out of the court, found him guilty. He was executed at Hull a short time after, but declared his innocence to the very last.

In less than twelve months after this event occurred, Brunell, the master of Jennings, was himself taken up for a robbery committed on a guest in his house, and the fact being proved on his trial, he was convicted and ordered for execution.

The approach of death brought on repentance; and repentance, confession. Brunell not only acknowledged having committed many highway robberies, but also the very one for which poor Jennings suffered. The account he gave was, that after robbing the gentleman, he arrived at home some time before him. That he found a man at home waiting, to whom he owned a small bill, and not having quite enough of money, he took out of the purse one guinea from the twenty he had just possessed himself of, to make up the sum, which he paid to the man, who then went away. Soon after the gentleman came to his house, and relating the account of the robbery, and that the guineas were marked, he became thunderstruck! Having paid one of them away, and not daring to apply for it again, as the affair of the robbery and of the marked guineas would soon become publicly known, detection, disgrace, and ruin appeared inevitable. Turning in his mind every way to escape, the thought of accusing and sacrificing poor Jennings at last struck him; and thus to his other crimes he added that of the murder of an innocent man.

Captain Death

In the month of December, 1756, the Terrible privateer, of twenty-six guns and two hundred men, commanded by Captain William Death, engaged the Grand Alexander, a French vessel of four hundred tons, twenty-two guns, and one hundred men; and after a smart fight of two hours and a half, in which Captain Death's brother and sixteen of his men were killed, he took her, and put forty men on board. A few days after, the Vengeance privateer of St Maloes, thirty-six guns and three hundred and sixty men, bore down upon her and retook the prize. The Vengeance and the prize then both attacked the Terrible, which was between them, and shot away their mainmast at the first broadside.

One of the most desperate engagements ever recorded ensued. It lasted one hour and a half. Mons. Bourdas, the French captain, his lieutenant, and two-thirds of his crew, on one side; and Captain Death, almost all his officers, and the greatest part of his crew, on the other side, were killed. The Terrible was ultimately taken and carried into St Maloes, in a shattered and frightful condition, having no more than twenty-six of the crew alive, of whom sixteen had lost legs or arms, and all the rest were otherwise wounded.

Distress Of A Robber

Shenstone was one day walking through his romantic retreat in company with his Delia (her real name was Wilmot), when a man rushed out of a thicket, and, presenting a pistol to his breast, demanded his money. Shenstone was surprised, and Delia fainted. 'Money,' said the robber, 'it is not worth struggling for; you cannot be poorer than I am.' 'Unhappy man!' exclaimed Shenstone, throwing his purse to him, 'take it and fly as quick as possible.' The man did so, threw his pistol in the water, and instantly disappeared.

Shenstone ordered his foot-boy to follow the robber, and observe where he went. In two hours the boy returned, and informed his master that he followed him to Hales-Owen, where he lived; that he went to the door of the house, and peeping through the key-hole, saw the man throw the purse on the ground, and say to his wife, 'Take the dear-bought price of my honesty.' Then, taking two of his children, one on each knee, he said to them,' I have ruined my soul to keep you from starving;' and immediately burst into a flood of tears. Shenstone, on hearing this, lost no time in enquiring the man's character; and found that he was a labourer in want, and a numerous family, but had the reputation of being honest and industrious. Shenstone went to his house; the poor man fell at his feet, and implored mercy. The poet took him home with him, and provided him with employment.

A Douglas

A captain of the name of Douglas, who commanded the Royal Oak when the Dutch sailed up the Medway, had received orders to defend his ship to the last extremity, but none to retire: and therefore when his ship was on fire, he chose rather to perish in her than quit his station, exclaiming heroically, 'A Douglas was never known to quit his post without orders!'

Bandit Of Goelnitz

A judge of the name of Helmanotn, in the department of Zips, sent a young female peasant with a sum of money to Goelnitz, a small town situated among the mountains. Not far from the village a countryman joined her, and demanded where was she going? The girl replied that she was journeying with a sum of 200 florins to Goelnitz. The countryman told her that he was going there also, and that they should travel together. At the wood, the countryman pursued a path which he told the girl would shorten their journey at least two leagues.

At length they arrived at the mouth of an excavation, which had once been worked as a mine; the countryman stopped short, and in a loud voice said to the girl, 'behold your grave; deliver me the money instantly.' The girl, trembling with fear, complied with his demand, and then entreated him to spare her life; the villain was inflexible, and he commanded her to prepare herself for death; the poor girl fell on her knees, and while in the act of supplicating for her life, the villain happened to turn away his head, when she sprang upon him, precipitating him into the cavity, and then ran and announced to the village what had happened.

Several of the inhabitants, provided with ladders, returned with her to the spot. They descended into the hole, and found the countryman dead, with the money which he had taken from the girl in his possession. Near him lay three dead female bodies in a state of putrefaction. It is probable that these were victims to the rapacity of the same villain. In a girdle which he had round his body, was discovered a sum of 800 florins in gold.

Adventures of Morgan, Prince of
Free-Booters: The Dark And Fetid Cellar

Continued from page 116...

Morgan, however, was not so easily discouraged, and did not yet despair of this rich capture. He had learnt that the galleon was destitute of water, of provisions, and even of sails and ropes; he conjectured that a ship so wretchedly supplied could not have gone any distance; and that she had probably taken refuge in some bay that was in the vicinity of Panama. He therefore detached four of his barks, which cruised for eight days in the circumjacent latitudes. Their cruise was fruitless; and the little flotilla returned without bringing in a single capture, and even without giving any hope of making a prize.

From Chagre the most satisfactory information was received. Every thing was quiet, and in the best order. The garrison had succeeded in taking a Spanish ship, which had unsuspectingly passed near the fort. She came from Carthagena, and there were found on board some chests full of emeralds. In consequence of this circumstance, Morgan determined to prolong his residence at Panama for some time: for he was not yet undeceived. He still flattered himself with the hope of ultimately meeting with this galleon, the object of general desire, and towards which his attention and his prayers were incessantly directed. In the mean time his men pursued their researches into the ruins of the consumed houses; within which treasure was most certainly concealed. In fact, some of the pirates did discover treasure in the wells and cellars, where it had been secreted by the Spaniards; while others were employed in burning the rich stuffs, in order to obtain the gold and silver with which they were embroidered.

Every apprehension of any attack from the Spaniards being thus removed, the free-booters settled themselves in such of the houses as were spared by the flames, and lived in perfect tranquillity, relying on the active vigilance of their strong patrols, who scoured the environs, and continually brought back booty and prisoners. In a short time they had seized upwards of one hundred mules richly laden, and more than two hundred persons of both sexes, who were tortured in the most barbarous manner, in order to compel them to disclose the places where they had concealed their precious effects. Many of them actually expired amidst these tortures; but their death affected their executioners so much the less, as it released them from several useless mouths, and a scarcity of provisions began to prevail. A few women of noble rank, who were gifted with external advantages, were treated with a degree of respect, which they could not expect from these ferocious men; but this was only when they yielded to their brutal desires. Those, on the contrary, who would not submit, experienced the most horrible treatment. Morgan himself set an example to his comrades. The following tale, which delineated that impetuous man in all his colours, deserves to be related.

Among those that were brought in, was a young and most lovely woman, of a mild and modest mien, but who possessed an elevated soul. She was the wife of an opulent merchant, who was then on a journey to Peru, whither his affairs called him. She was flying with her parents when she was detained by the free-booters. The moment Morgan beheld her, he destined her for his pleasures. At first she was treated with respect and separated from the rest of the prisoners; although she with tears besought him to spare her this distinction, more formidable than flattering. He gave her an apartment in his dwelling, together with negroes to attend, and supped with her from his own table. He even permitted the captive Spanish women to visit her. She was astonished at this treatment; as the free-booters had been represented to her, as well as to her country women, as a kind of monsters, equally hideous in their forms as their character was odious. It is related by these, who have transmitted to us the particulars of this event, that a Spanish woman exclaimed with surprise, who beheld them for the first time, – 'O Holy Mary! These robbers are in every respect like our Spaniards!'

At first the heroine of this little romance did not suspect that her charms were the cause of such a delicate and unexpected reception. She shortly, however, learnt the real design of this treatment. Morgan gave her three days to consider whether she would voluntarily yield to the passion she had inspired. He laid at her feet whatever was most valuable of his booty, either in gold, pearls, or diamonds. But she rejected all his presents; and, after steadfastly refusing the most pressing entreaties, she told him with the greatest firmness, 'My life is in your hands; but you shall exercise no dominion over my body until my soul is separated from it.' As she uttered these words, she drew forth a dagger, which she had concealed, but which was instantly taken from her. The ferocious Morgan, incapable of any sentiment of generosity, a stranger to every kind of virtue, caused her clothes to be torn off, and cast her naked into a dark and fetid cellar, where she was supplied with only the grossest food, and in such small quantities as were scarcely sufficient to prolong her melancholy days.

… Morgan began now to think seriously of returning [home]. After three weeks' residence at Panama, the freebooters abandoned that city, or rather the situation at which it had formerly occupied. The booty, which consisted principally of gold, silver, and jewels (for no other articles were portable), was laden upon one hundred and seventy-five beasts of burden, by the side of which upwards of six hundred prisoners, men, women, and children, inhabitants as well as slaves, were compelled to walk on foot. Ignorant of the place of their destination, and exhausted by hunger and fatigue, these unfortunate persons abandoned themselves to lamentations, which would have excited compassion in the breasts of every one but their ferocious conductors, whom they conjured upon their knees to grant them the favour of returning to the pile of ashes which had been their country. Morgan replied that he would grant them permission, provided they would produce money for their ransom. Such a condition was equivalent to a refusal. The captives, however, waited four days, for the return of some ecclesiastics, whom they had dispatched for the purpose of collecting, if it were possible, the sum required by the insatiable Morgan.

As they did not return, the pirates resumed their march, violently goading and beating, even to death, such as did not walk with sufficient speed. In this group of unfortunates were mothers, carrying infants at their breasts; and who, being themselves destitute of sustenance, could not yield a single drop of milk to support their offspring; and among them was the lovely woman already noticed, for whose liberty Morgan required a ransom of thirty thousand piasters. To raise that sum, she had sent two monks to a particular spot, whence they returned with the money she had expected. But, instead of employing it in her deliverance, they appropriated it to the redeeming of some other prisoners who were their friends. This atrocious treachery soon became known, and increased the interest which the free-booters took in the fate of the victim. Morgan himself could not suppress an emotion of pity; he interrogated the other monastics whom he was dragging along, respecting the transaction; which being fully proved, he at length released his beauteous captive, but detained all the monks by way of retaliation, in order to atone for the perfidy of their brethren. They also succeeded in procuring their ransom; and, during their march, many other prisoners had the same good fortune; but the majority, not being able to obtain the sum exacted for their ransom, were obliged to continue their route.

To be continued…

The Outlaw of Calabria

One of the most celebrated leaders of the bands of brigands which infested Calabria and the Abruzzi, in 1817, was the priest of Ciro Annichiarico, who, though born of respectable parents, and bred to the ecclesiastical profession, abandoned himself to crime at an early period of his life. He began his infamous career by killing a young man of the Motolesi family, in a fit of jealousy. His insatiable hatred pursued every member of the family, and exterminated them one after the other, with the exception of a single individual who succeeded in evading his search, and who lived shut up in his house for several years, without ever daring to go out. This unfortunate being thought that a snare was laid for him, when people came to tell him of the imprisonment, and shortly after the death of his enemy; and it was with difficulty that he was induced to quit his retreat.

Ciro, condemned for the murder of Motolesi to fifteen years of chains or exile, by the tribunal of Lecce, remained there in prison for four years, when he made his escape. It was then that he began to lead a vagabond life, which was stained by the most atrocious crimes. At Eartano, he penetrated with his accomplices into one of the first houses of the place, massacred the mistress and all her attendants, and carried off ninety-six thousand ducats. He became in correspondence with all the hired brigands; and whoever wished to get rid of an enemy had only to address himself to Ciro. On being asked by captain Montori, reporter of the commission which condemned him, how many persons he had killed with his own hand, he carelessly answered, 'Who can remember? they will be between sixty and seventy.' One of his companions, Occhiolupo, confessed to seventeen; the two brothers, Francesco and Vito Serio, to twenty-three; so that these four ruffians alone had assassinated upwards of a hundred!

The activity of Ciro was as astonishing as his artifice and intrepidity. He handled his musket and managed his horse to perfection; and as he was always extremely well mounted, he found concealment and support, either through fear or inclination, every where. He succeeded in escaping from the hands of the soldiers by forced marches of thirty or forty miles, even when confidential spies had discovered his place of concealment but a few hours before. The singular good fortune of his being able to extricate himself from the most imminent dangers, acquired for him the reputation of a necromancer, upon whom ordinary means of attack had no power among the people, and he neglected nothing that could confirm this idea, and increase the sort of spell it produced on the peasants. They dared not execrate or even blame him in his absence, so firmly were they persuaded that his demons would inform him of it.

Ciro put himself at the head of two associations of most desperate character, the Patrioti Europei, and the Decisi. The institution of the Decisi, or decided, was of the most horrible nature. They kept a register of the victims they immolated; and had what they called a director of funeral ceremonies, for they slaughtered with method and solemnity. As soon as the detachments employed in this service, found it convenient to effect their purpose, at the first blast of the trumpet they unsheathed their poignards; at the second blast, they aimed them at their victim; at the third, they gradually brought their weapons towards his breast; and at the forth signal, plunged them into their bodies.

In 1817, these associations had become so formidable, that General Church was sent with an army to exterminate them; but with men linked by such ties, a person of Ciro's determined character was not to be put down easily. He therefore made the most desperate efforts to defend himself. At length, worn out by fatigue, Ciro and three companions, Vito de Cesare, Giovanni Palmieri, and Michele Cuppoli, had taken refuge in Scaserba, to repose themselves for a few hours. He had previously provided this, and all the farm-houses of the district, with ammunition and some provisions. When he saw the militia of S. Marzano marching against him, he appeared very little alarmed, and thought he could very easily cut through their ranks. He shot the first man dead who came within range of his musket. This delay cost him dear; the militia sent information to Lieutenant

Fonsmore, stationed at the Castelli, a strong position between Crottaglie and Francavilla. This officer hastened to the spot with forty men.

On seeing him approach, Ciro perceived that a vigorous attack was to be made. He shut up the people of the Masseria in the straw magazine, and put the key in his pocket. He took away the ladder from the tower, and loaded, with the aid of his companions, all the guns, of which he had a good number.

Next morning, Major Bianchi proceeded in person to Scaserba, and besieged Ciro, with one hundred and thirty soldiers, while a body of the militia were placed at some distance. He attempted to escape in the night, but the neighing of a horse made him suspect that some cavalry had arrived, whose pursuit it would be impossible to elude. He retired, after having killed, with a pistol shot, a Voltigeur, stationed under the wall which he attempted to scale. He again shut himself up in his tower, and employed himself till morning in making cartridges. At day-break, the besiegers tried to burst open the wooden gate of the outer wall; Ciro and his men repulsed the assailants by a well-directed fire; they killed five and wounded fourteen men.

A barrel of oil was brought, in order to burn the door. The first man who set fire to it was shot through the heart. A four-pounder, which had been conveyed to the place, was pointed against the roof of the tower. Several of this calibre had been contrived to be easily dismounted from their carriages, and transported on mules. This little piece produced great effect, and the tiles and brick which fell, forced Ciro to descend from the second to the first floor. After some deliberations with his companions, he demanded to speak with General Church, who he believed was in the neighbourhood; then to the Duke of Jasi, who was also absent; at last, he resolved to capitulate with Major Bianchi. He addressed the besiegers, and threw some bread. Major Bianchi promised that he should not be maltreated by the soldiers. He descended the ladder, opened the door of the tower, and presented himself with these words, 'Here I am, Don Ciro!'

He begged them to give him some water to quench his thirst, and desired them to liberate the farmer and his family, who had been shut up all this time in the straw magazine. He declared that they were innocent, and distributed money amongst them. He suffered himself to be searched and bound patiently; some poison was found on him, which he said his companions had prevented him from taking. In prison, he appeared to be interested for the fate of some of his partisans, begging that they might not be persecuted, and declaring that they had been forced to do what they had done. He had entertained some hope till the moment when he was placed before the Council of War, and refused permission to speak to General Church. He was condemned to death. On his arrival at the place of execution, Ciro wished to remain standing, but was told to kneel; he did so, presenting his breast. He was then informed that malefactors like himself were shot with their backs towards the soldiers; he submitted, at the same time advising a priest, who persisted in remaining near him, to withdraw, so as not to expose himself.

Twenty-one balls took effect, four in the head, yet he still breathed and muttered in his throat: the twenty-second put an end to him. This fact is confirmed by all the officers and soldiers present at his death. 'As soon as we perceived,' said a soldier very gravely, 'that he was enchanted, we loaded his own musket with a silver ball, and this destroyed the spell.' It will easily be supposed that the people, who always attributed to him supernatural powers, were confirmed in their belief by this tenacity of life which they considered miraculous.

King James IV And The Scottish Banditti

During the early part of his reign almost the whole of the country was infested (as it had been during the reigns of his predecessors) with innumerable hordes of banditti and robbers; who, having taken up their residence in the dark caverns and gloomy forests of the Highlands, often conjured together and sallied forth in considerable numbers upon the unguarded husbandman and villager, or benighted and unwary traveller. Many dreadful anecdotes are upon record relative to these lawless bands, who having grown powerful and insolent, in consequence of the supineness or insufficiency of the government, which, during those dark days, possessed little real power – even bearded the monarch in his very palace.

Their criminal offences at last arrived at such a pitch, that king James, soon after his accession to the throne, resolved, if possible, utterly to extirpate them. This he nearly accomplished – but the task was too Herculean for him to effect; what he left undone, his successor fully completed; and we consequently hear but little of these freebooters after this period. The daring deeds, dreadful crimes, and bloody cruelties, of which they were guilty, appear to have equalled in monstrosity those committed by the banditti of the Alps, the Carbonari of Italy, or the Forestmen of Ireland. For their lawless depredations the rocky glens, deep ravines, gloomy forests, and yawning chasms of the Highlands of Scotland were well suited; and the strong holds which they possessed, and which were always guarded with the most wary caution, rendered their abodes inaccessible to the stranger.

King James IV possessed an innate courage which rendered him superior to every feeling of fear or terror; and in the early part of his government, perceiving the increasing power of these desperadoes, and that their deeds became more fearful and glaring, he determined at every risk to bring them to that justice which had so long been exerted for the removal of the evil. For this purpose he would wander disguised for days among the gloomy woods and recesses of the Highland mountains, and make such observations as were necessary for the fulfilment of this design. In the course of these lonely excursions, he often fell into dangerous snares and fearful perils, from which nothing but his own extraordinary boldness, presence of mind, and promptitude of execution could possibly extricate him.

He was once overtaken by a violent storm of thunder and lightning, and the night being pitchy dark, excepting when the vivid gleam shed a flickering light over the dreary wastes of the forest, he was compelled to take shelter in a cavern near Wemys, which is one of the most remarkable antiquities of Scotland. Having advanced a considerable way into it, the king discovered a number of men and women of uncouth dress and appearance ready to begin to roast a sheep, by way of supper. From their place of abode, and mysterious and cautious whispers he began to suspect that he had not fallen into the best of company; but, as it was too late to retreat, he requested hospitality till the storm was over. They granted it, and, after some consultations by signs, they invited the monarch, whom they did not know, to sit down, and take part with them. They were a band of these outlawed desperadoes whose deeds filled every heart with terror. As soon as they had finished their repast, one of them presented a plate, upon which two daggers were placed in the form of a St Andrew's cross, telling the king, at the same time, that this was the dessert which they always served to strangers; that he must choose one of the daggers, and combat with him whom the company should appoint to attack him. The king did not lose his presence of mind, but instantly seized the two daggers, one in each hand, and plunged them into the hearts of the two robbers who were next to him; and running full speed to the mouth of the cavern, he escaped from their pursuit, through the obscurity of the night, and the horrors of the storm. The king arrived safe at his residence, and without delay deputed a sturdy band to seize upon these outlaws.– This was accordingly done, and the whole of them were hanged without mercy.

Adventures of Morgan, Prince Of Free-Booters
– A Wicked End To A Long Career

Continued from page 132...
They halted about half-way from Chagre; when every free-booter was called upon to affirm by oath, that he had not appropriated to himself the slightest portion of the plunder.

Notwithstanding the oath was taken, the suspicious Morgan demanded that the clothes and portmanteaus of the whole troop should be minutely examined, one after another. In order to obviate any thing that might be offensive in these commands, he underwent an examination first; and lest any thing should escape the strict search to which he himself had submitted, he stripped off his own boots. From this rigorous inquiry none of his companions in arms durst shrink, although very many of them, particularly the French, murmured loudly with much bitterness at such a proceeding.

The execution of the chieftain's orders was committed to the officers, who discharged them with extreme severity. Even the fusees were taken to pieces, lest any precious stones should have been secreted between the iron and the stocks. This excessive mistrust excited the indignation of some of the free-booters to such a degree, that they threatened Morgan with death; but the majority of voices was against them, and supported a measure which the common interest seemed to require. In this point of view, every thing was lawful; every thing was commanded on one part, and tolerated on the other. Morgan, who knew how to unite address with imperious arrogance on some occasions, had recommended to the officers to take silently away the concealed articles their inquiries might have discovered, without divulging the transgressors of the law. These manoeuvres produced the desired effect, and the general tranquillity was not disturbed.

At length, on the 9th of March, 1671, the free-booters reached Chagre, where they found all things in tolerable order, excepting that most of their comrades had expired for want of proper assistance. From Chagre Morgan sent all his prisoners in a ship to Porto Bello, which city he threatened with total destruction, unless it was redeemed with a very heavy ransom. To this requisition it was answered, that not a single halfpenny would be given; and consequently that he might do whatever he pleased. Morgan's threats were never in vain. He caused all the cannon belonging to the fort to be conveyed on board his own ship, with which he destroyed the walls, caused the houses to be burnt, and destroyed every thing which could not possibly be carried away.

The expedition was now terminated; and it only remained to make a division of the booty, which was valued at four hundred and forty-three thousand two hundred lbs. weight of silver, at a rate of ten piasters per pound. On this occasion Morgan behaved like a shameless robber towards those very comrades who had so quietly submitted to his examination, and who had brought into the common chest every thing they could have appropriated to themselves, to his detriment. He allowed the most flagitious spoiliations, causing a vast quantity of precious stones to be set apart for his own use; so that each of his companions in arms, or rather each of his accomplices in all his tortures and cruelties, received, as a reward for so many fatigues and dangers, only to the value of two hundred piasters for his own share.

The free-booters expressed their displeasure in violent murmurs; they reproached Morgan to his face for not bringing the most precious articles into the general mass, and charged him with applying them to his own use exclusively. The charge was certainly well-founded; a great number of articles, which many of the pirates had brought in, having disappeared at the time of making the division. To these complaints were added others of equal weight; which would, at some moment or other, excite a mutiny: but the faithless chieftain was not at all disposed to grant any satisfaction to the malcontents. He did not, however, wait for the breaking out of the rebellion; and in order to reconcile every difference, he went secretly on board his own ship, and set sail with three other vessels, whose commanders had been equally dishonest as himself with regard to booty, and who were in consequence devoted to him. The remainder of the fleet was left behind. Furious at finding themselves so shamefully abandoned, the other free-booters determined to pursue Morgan, and immediately attack him; but they were entirely destitute of provisions, and every other necessary article. They were therefore obliged to dispose themselves into small troops, in order to procure sustenance by pillaging the coast of Costarica, and afterwards resume their route from different quarters. But this plan was frustrated by a variety of accidents which occurred; nor did they succeed in re-entering Jamaica till a long time had elapsed, and after they had encountered infinite difficulties.

Notwithstanding his fortunate exploits and his laborious exertions, Morgan did not yet think of relinquishing the stormy profession of piracy; and, although he had lately conducted himself so unfairly towards his comrades, still he was certain to meet with others who would co-operate in his future expeditions. He therefore conceived a new project, which entered into all his views, and was to render his successes more solid. He proposed to convey a certain number of men to the island of St Catherine, to fortify it carefully, and to render it the residence of the free-booters. This plan was on the eve of being carried into execution, when an English ship of the line arrived at Jamaica with dispatches, which were a thunderbolt to the free-booters. The governor of the colony was recalled home to answer for the protection he had given those 'blood-thirsty and plundering rascals,' and the officer who was to succeed him was then on board. No sooner had the latter landed, then he published, in every port under British dominion, the king of England's determination to live for the future in a good understanding with the Spanish monarch and his subjects in America. And a very severe prohibition was therefore issued, forbidding any free-booter to quit Jamaica with the design of attacking the Spanish possessions.

The English pirates were at sea when this news arrived; they were unwilling to incur the risk of a return, lest they should lose all their booty, in consequence of this change in the political arrangements. For some time, therefore, they were obliged to wander at the pleasure of the winds, and were fortunate enough to reach the French island of Tortuga, the ancient refuge of the pirates, and the only place in the West Indian seas which now continued open to them.

From this time Morgan relinquished all his vast projects, and withdrew from this theatre of robbery, on which he had acted so principal a part. To that fierce activity which seemed to be his peculiar element, succeeded a peaceful and tranquil life. He settled at Jamaica, where he was promoted to the most distinguished offices; and enjoyed, in perfect security, those riches which had cost his unfortunate victims so many tears, and so much bloodshed; but which did not produce any remorse whatsoever in his callous heart.

More *Tales from the* *Terrific Register*...

The Book of Wonders
EDITED BY CATE LUDLOW

Contained herein you will find giants, horned children, babies brought up by wolves, uncanny dreams, devils, and attacks by cannibals, snakes, crocodiles, and bears.

978 07524 5265 4

The Book of Murder
EDITED BY CATE LUDLOW

Including dreadful executions, foul tortures and notorious killers, this volume will chill all but the sturdiest hearts.

978 07524 5266 1

The Book of Ghosts
EDITED BY CATE LUDLOW

The reader will find reports of apparitions and premonitions of all kinds, extraordinary instances of second sight, and visitations from spirits.

978 07524 5416 0

The Book of London
EDITED BY CATE LUDLOW

With gripping accounts of fires, floods, executions and the Great Plague, this selection will delight all those who know and love the city.

978 07524 5264 7

Visit our website and discover thousands of other History Press books.
www.thehistorypress.co.uk

The History Press